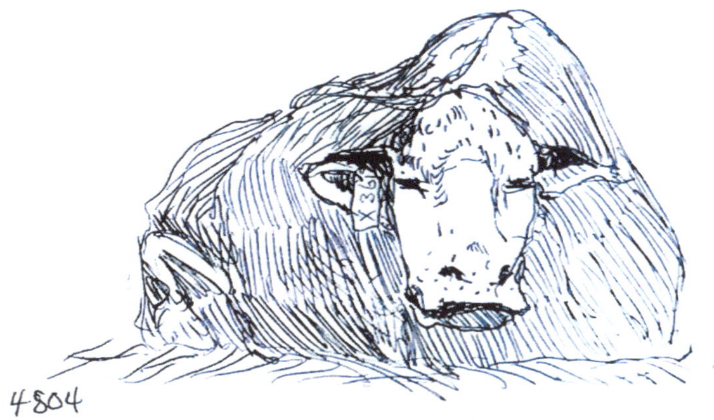

ON DRAWING TEN THOUSAND THINGS

Gwen Diehn

Published on the occasion of the exhibition

DRAWING TEN THOUSAND THINGS

at Asheville BookWorks - January 26 through March 31, 2018

Design by Laura Ladendorf • Digital Imaging by Gwen Diehn

Gwen Diehn's prints, drawings and artists' books have been exhibited internationally and are in many collections, including the National Museum of Women in the Arts, Washington, DC. She has taught art at the college level and in short courses and workshops for many years. She is the author of several Sterling/Lark books, including *Simple Printmaking* (2000), *Real Life Journals* (*Journal Your Way* paperback title) (2010), and *The Complete Decorated Journals* (2013).

ISBN: 978-0-692-99316-3

DRAWING TEN THOUSAND THINGS

A FRIEND SENT ME A SKETCH SHE HAD MADE IN A RESTAURANT. On the wall behind a man with a plaited beard was written: "You cannot learn to draw until you have drawn the ten thousand things." Curious, I mentioned the quote to another friend, who told me that the term Ten Thousand Things refers to the myriad, countless manifestations of the Universal (or Tao or energy or God or whatever term one uses for the mysterious animating force of the universe).

I was experienced in drawing and the teaching of drawing, but I wondered what effect drawing and numbering ten thousand things would have on my drawings, on my practice, on my life in general. And so, without further deliberation, I picked up my then-current sketchbook and favorite pen and headed out to the mountain trail at the end of my road to see what I could see.

On that June afternoon I draw quickly one of the first daylilies of the season, a mulch pile in the old apple orchard at the beginning of the trail, a bird on a wire, an imma-ture apple on a branch. And then I heard a quiet crash. I turned just in time to see a large orange and white foxtail disappear into some brush across the trail from the orchard. I scrawled an image of the bounding fox—the first fox I had ever seen on this trail. That seemed like a good omen for the project. I went home and posted the drawings on my blog (http://real-life-journals.blogspot.com) along with a brief state-ment of my intention.

Thus I continued, day after day, line by line, step by step without looking back or ahead for four years. When on a sunny morning in June, exactly four years after starting the project, I spotted a hen scratching in the dust and stopped to draw her dancing motion, I wrote the number 10,000.

I was interested in how pleasurable the practice was. I soon got into a rhythm of making between seven and ten drawings a day. Occasionally I needed to draw scenes or groups or illuminated maps; since I was the rule-maker, I decided it was fine to count the somewhat discreet parts of these compositions as individual things. Very occasionally I skipped a day, and sometimes I drew twenty things in a single day. Once my sketchbook with around a hundred drawings in it was stolen along with my bag in Barcelona. I estimated the number of stolen drawings and jotted it down in the sequence when I picked up a new sketchbook. I generally posted catch-up blog posts when I returned home from traveling—giving myself a vacation from blogging but not wanting a vacation from drawing.

As time went on I thought less, and then not at all, while drawing. It felt like a meditation. My eyes relaxed and my vision improved to the point that I no longer wear glasses. I relaxed into the connectedness of everything, the fascination of everything. I often researched things I had never seen before—the cleistogamous marriage of violets, the language of venery, caput mortuum in early spring, the elegance and economy of seeds and nuts, frost heaves, facial expressions, shoes in Penn Station in winter viewed from the floor of the Amtrak waiting room. Often I would look at a drawing and wonder how I had done it. It seemed to have drawn itself.

In sum, I would make a change to the statement that started me off on this project: You cannot *know* the ten thousand things until you have drawn them. And in the process you will have learned much about seeing and drawing.

OCTOBER, 2017

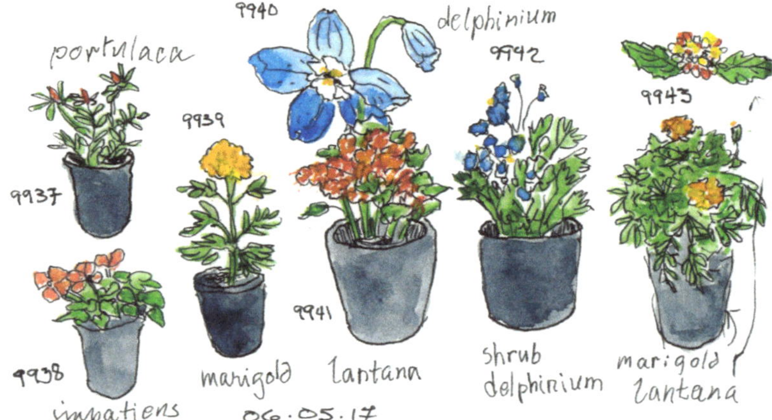

4

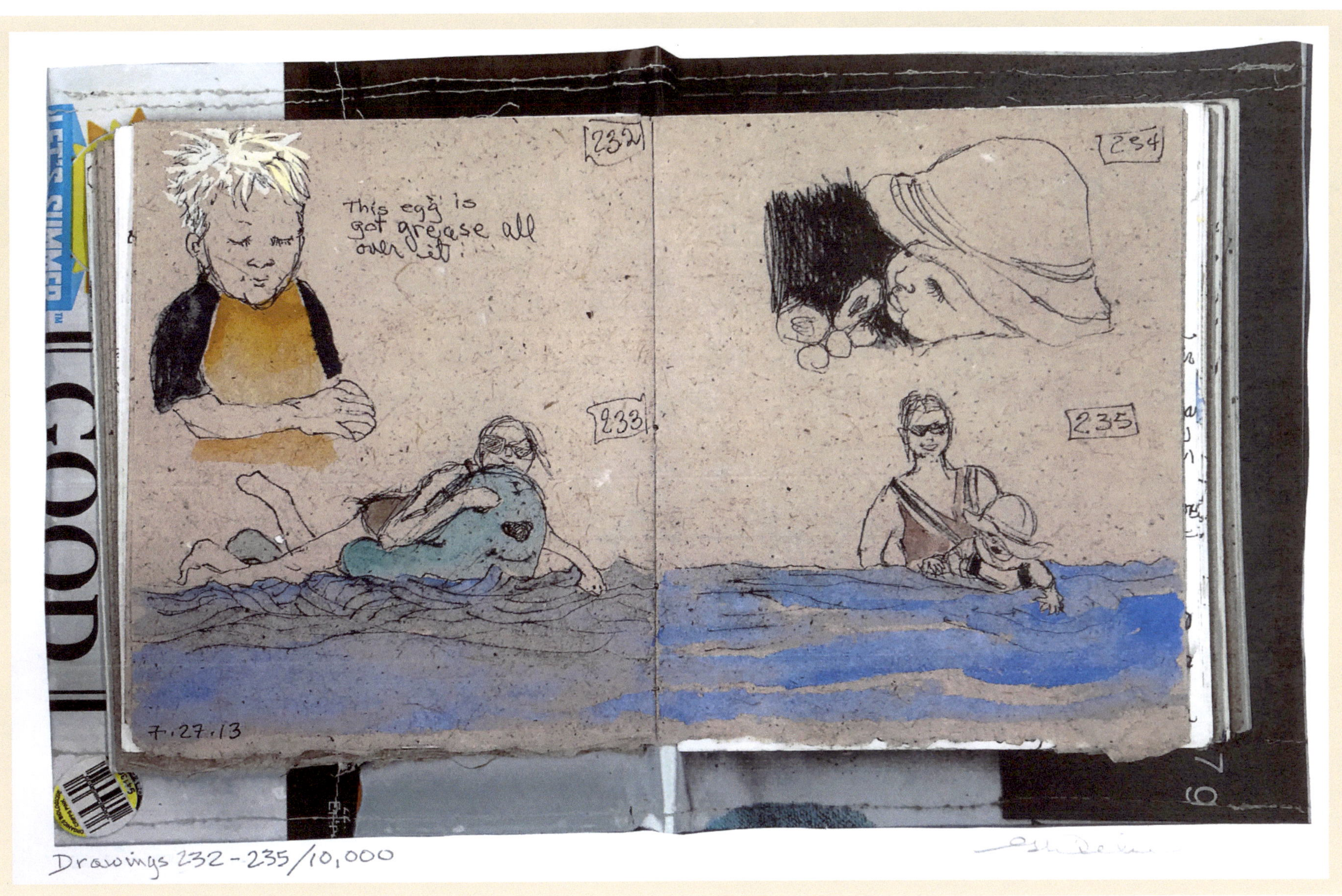

Drawings 232 - 235/10,000

5

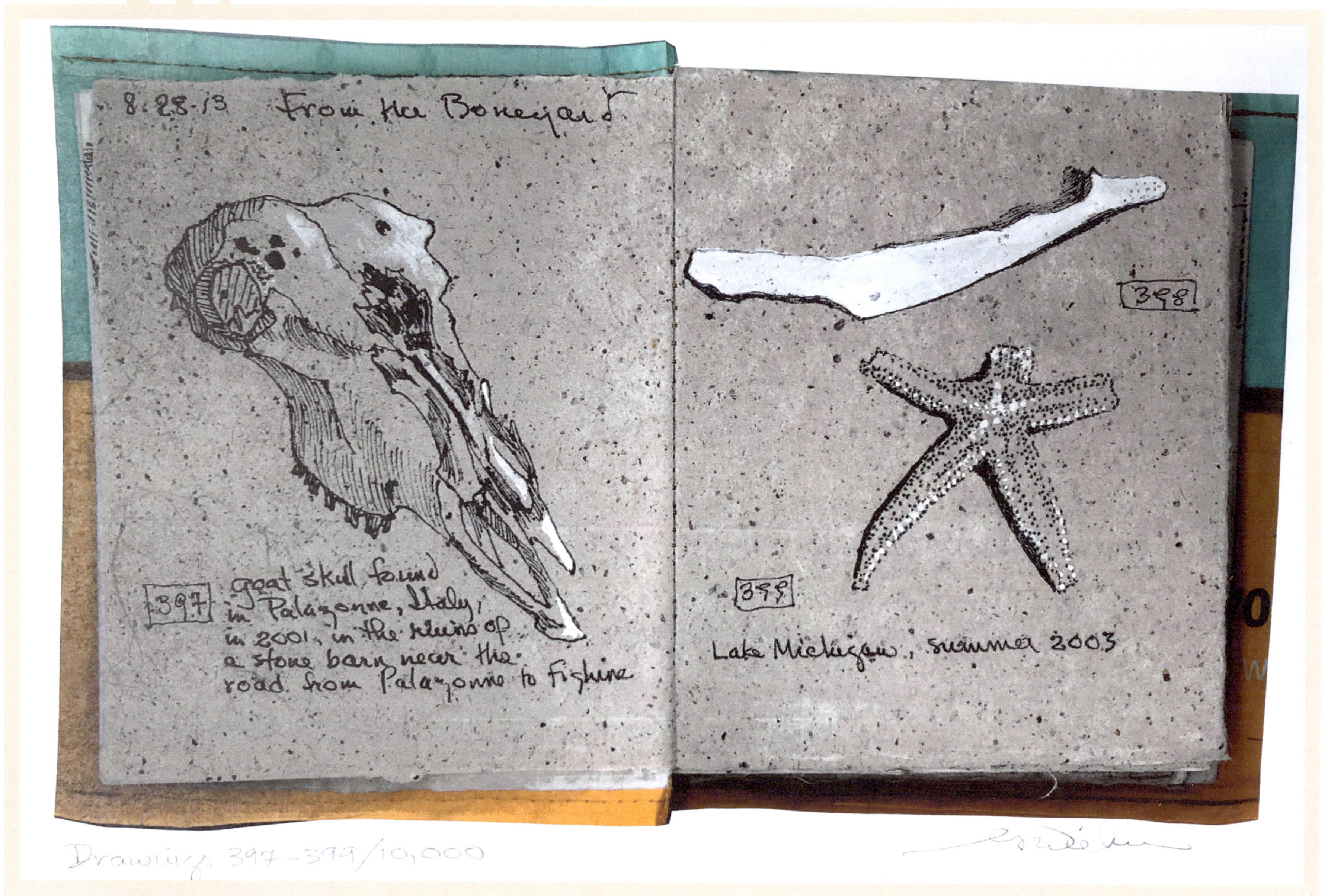

Drawings 397-399/10,000

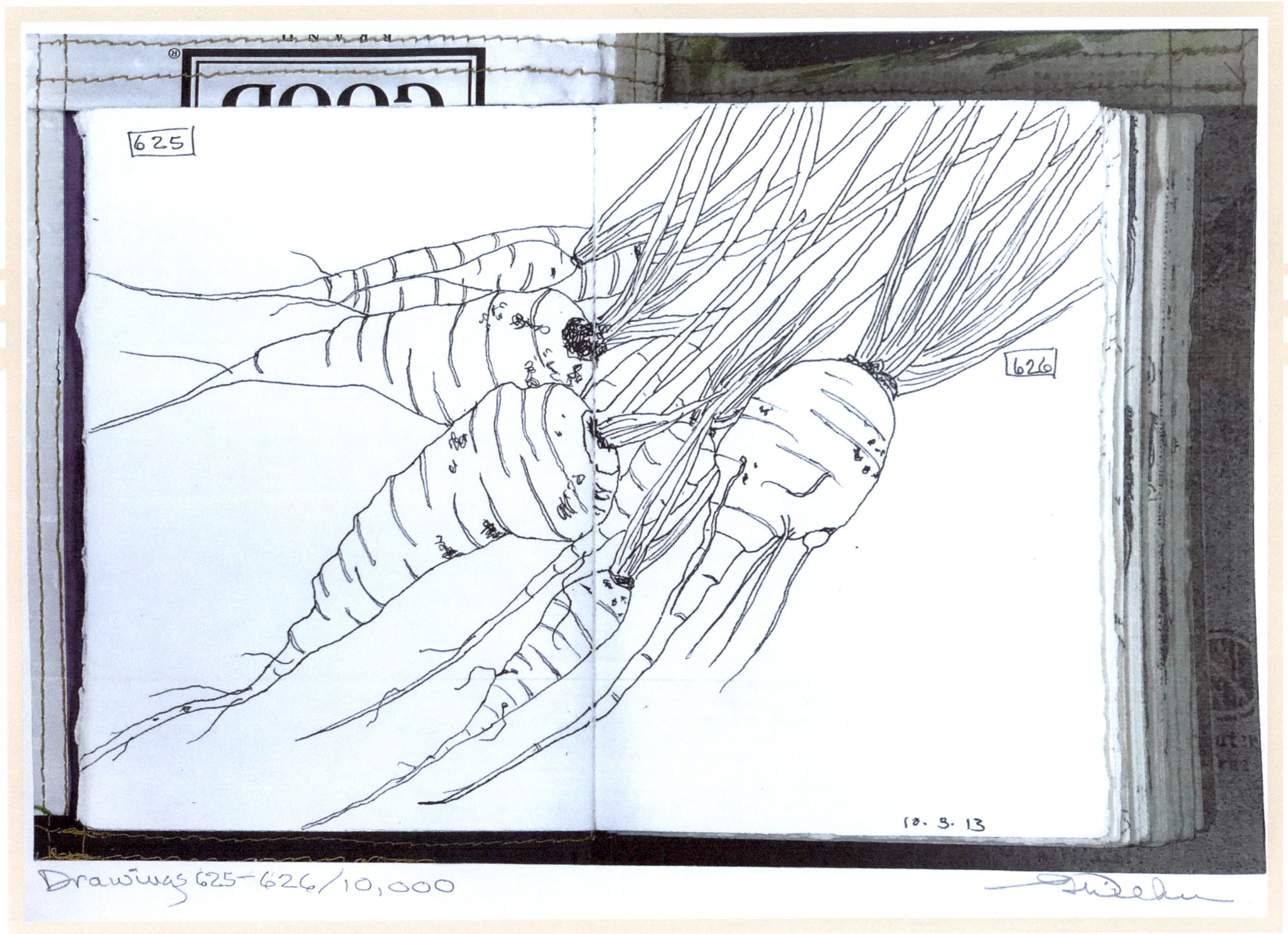

Drawings 625-626/10,000

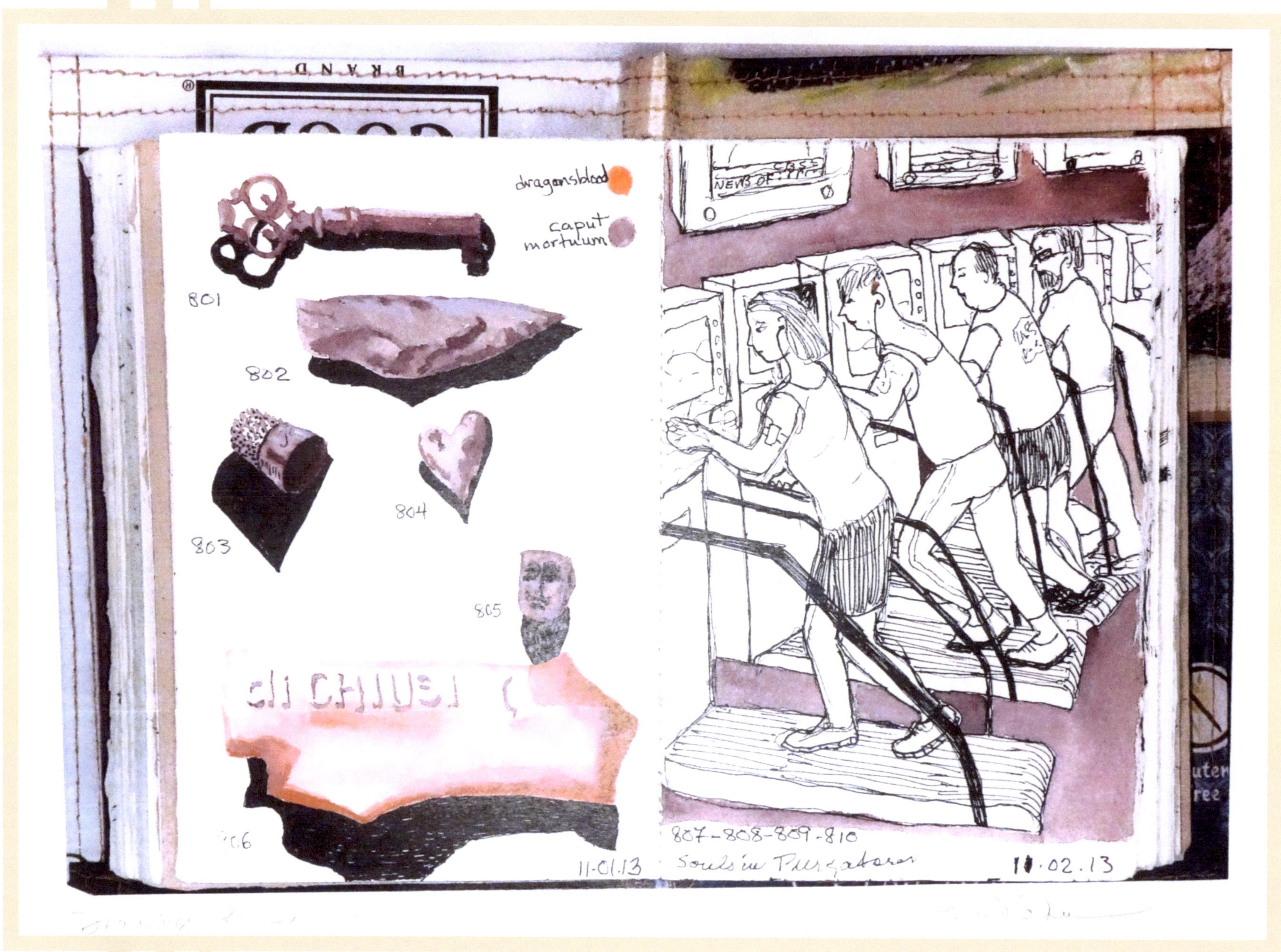
BRAND
GOOD
dragonsblood
caput
mortulum
801
802
803
804
805
806
di CHIUSI
11·01·13
807-808-809-810
Souls in Purgatory
11·02·13

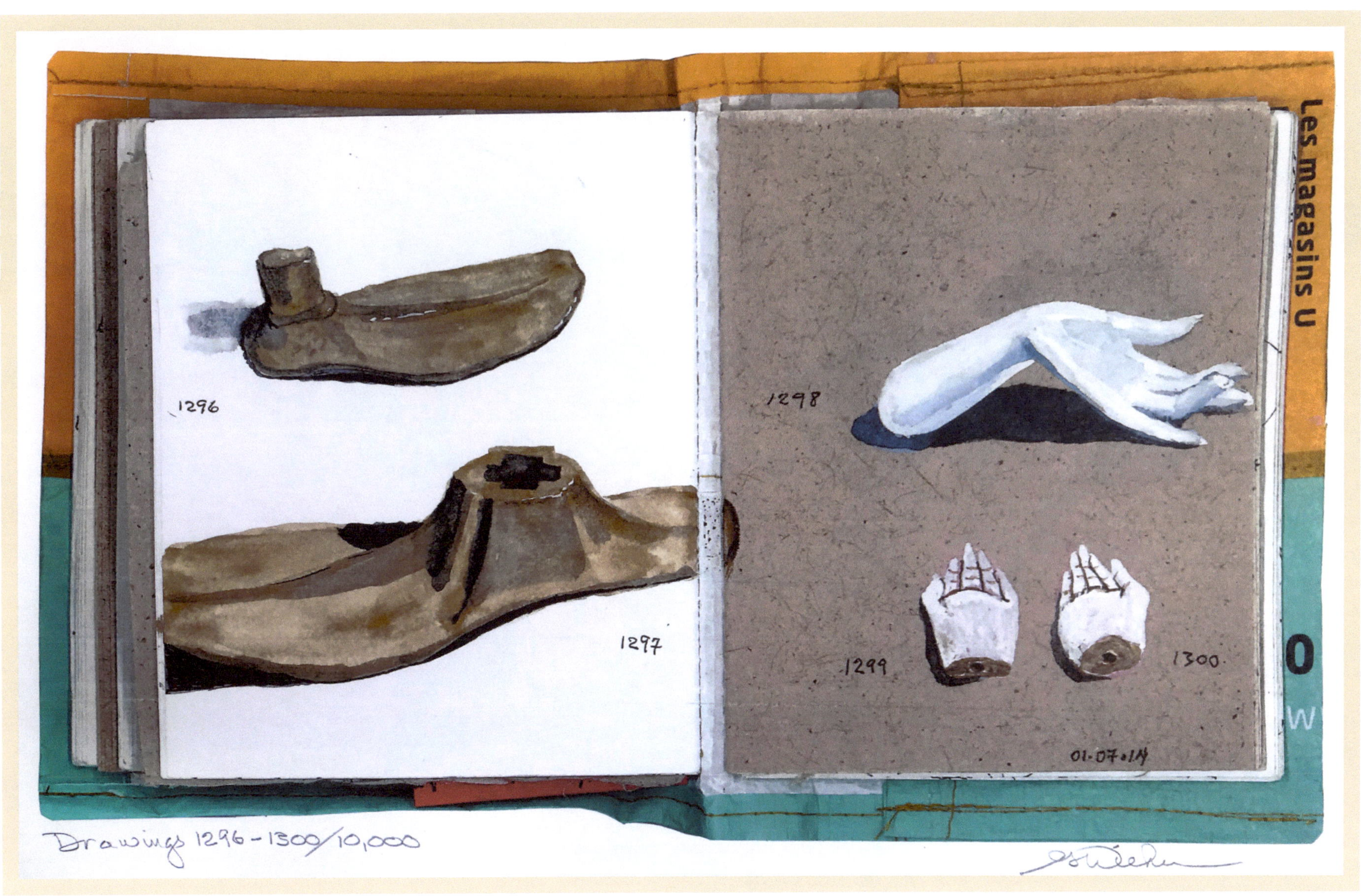

Drawings 1296–1300/10,000

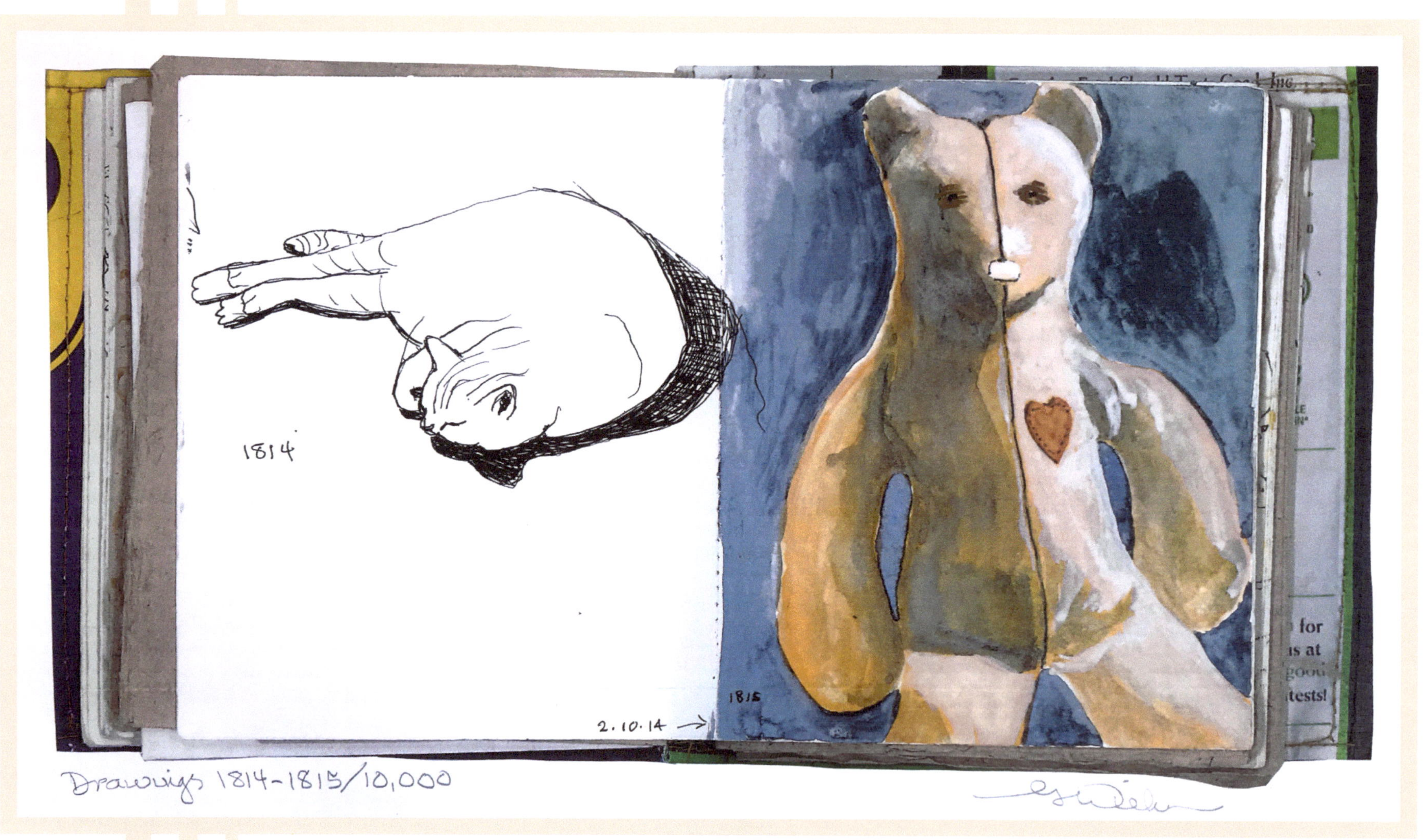

Drawings 1814-1815/10,000

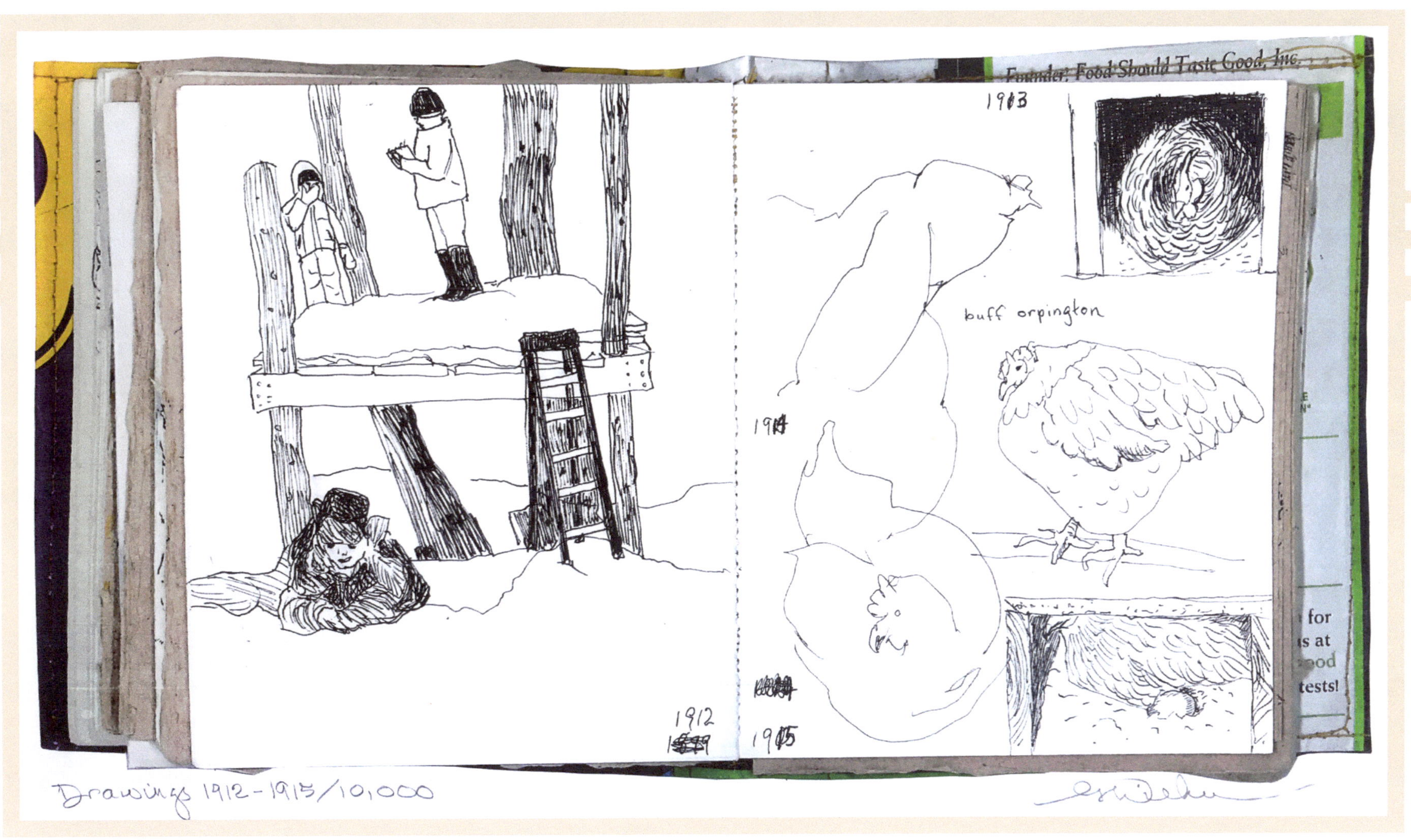

Drawings 1912–1915/10,000

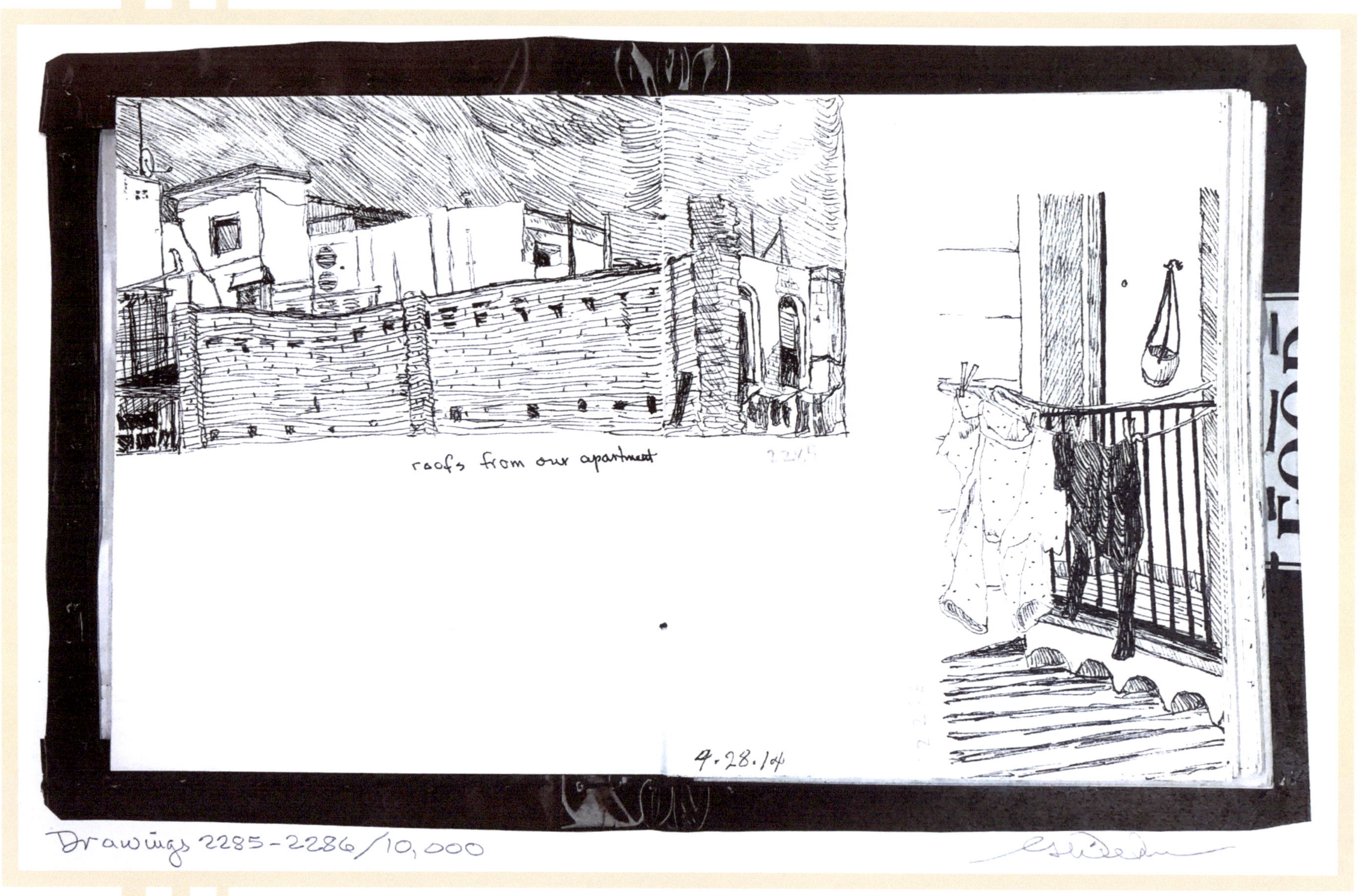

Drawings 2285-2286/10,000

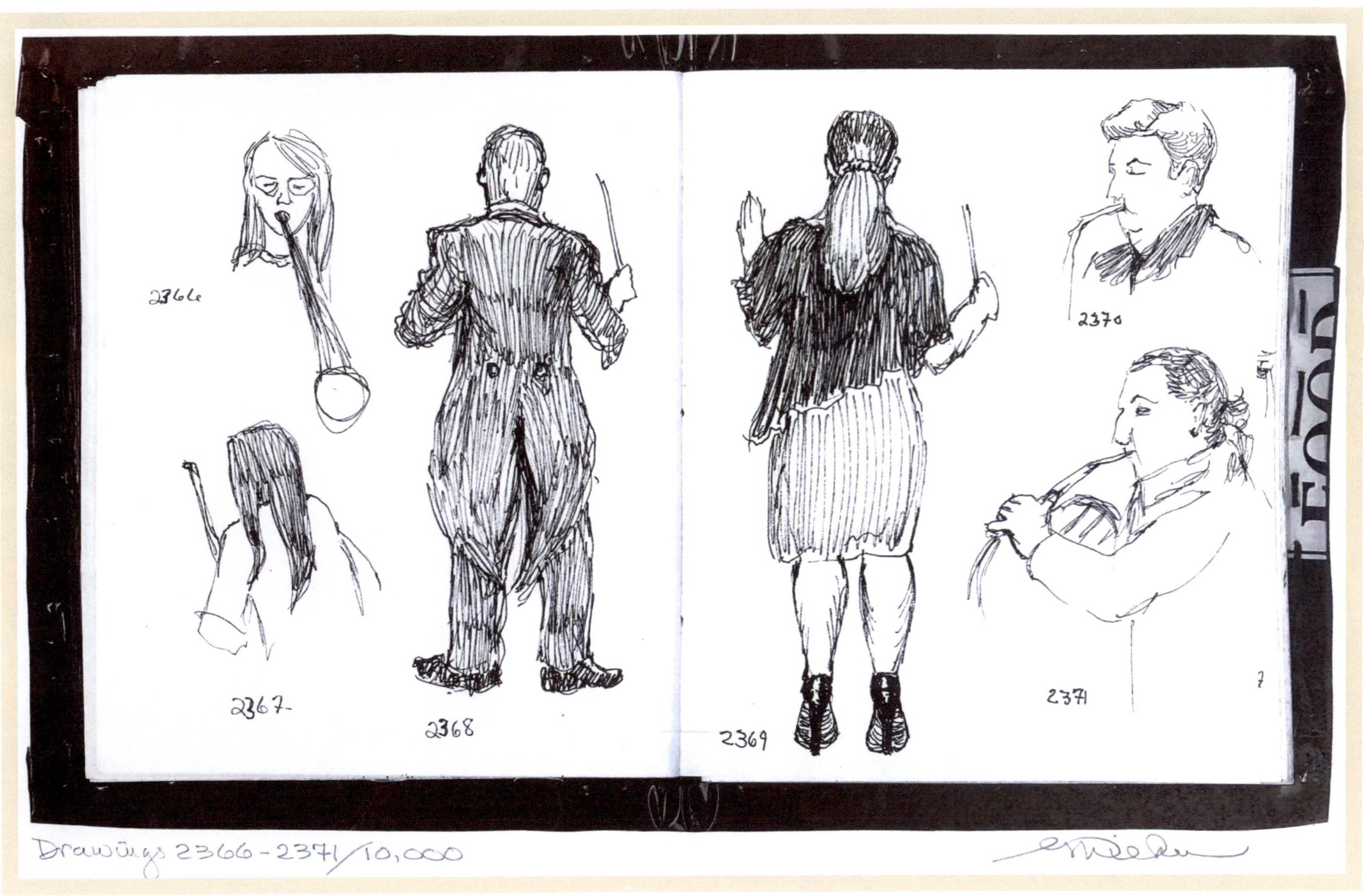

Drawings 2366 – 2371/10,000

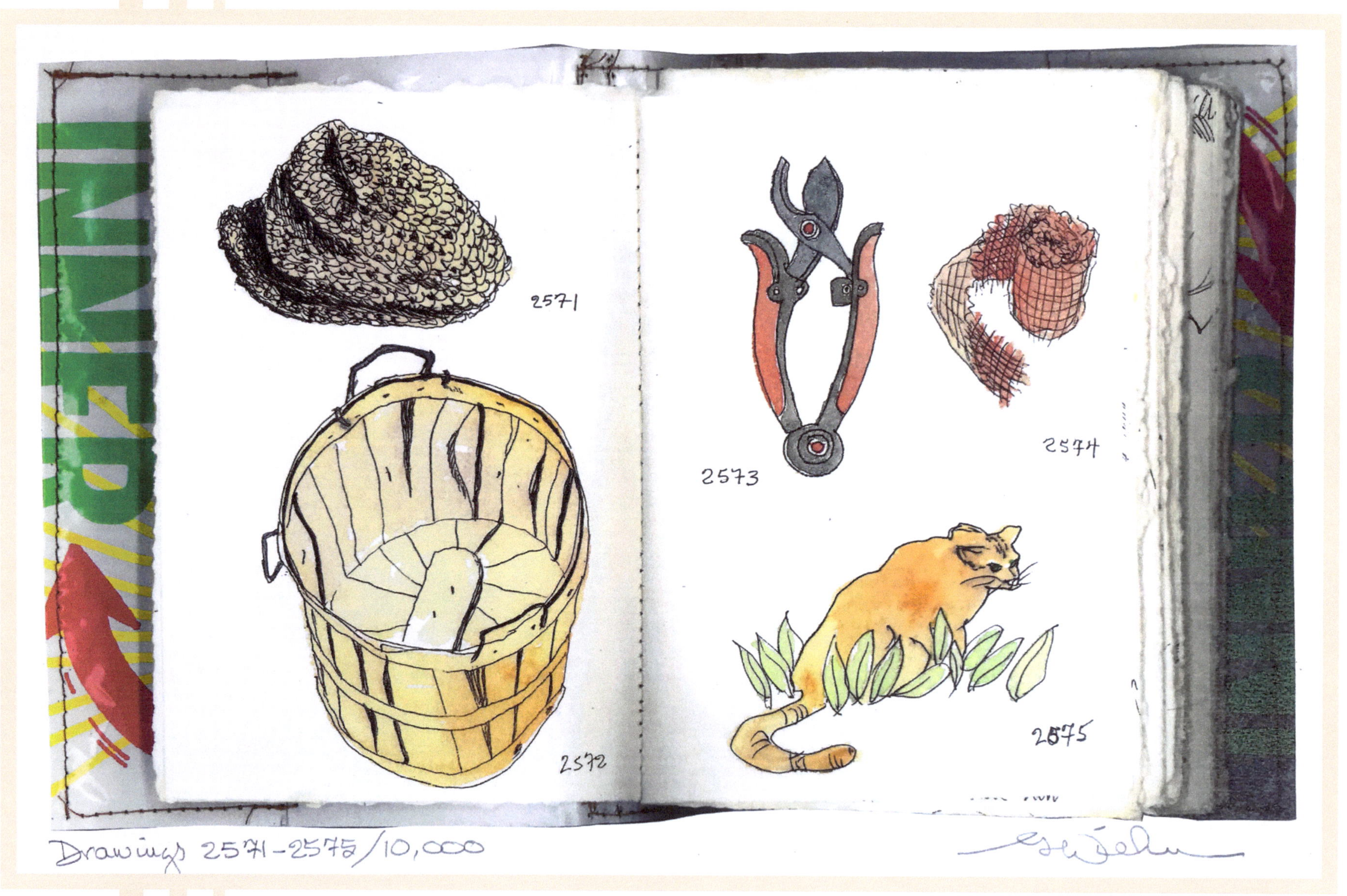

2571
2572
2573
2574
2575
Drawings 2571-2575/10,000

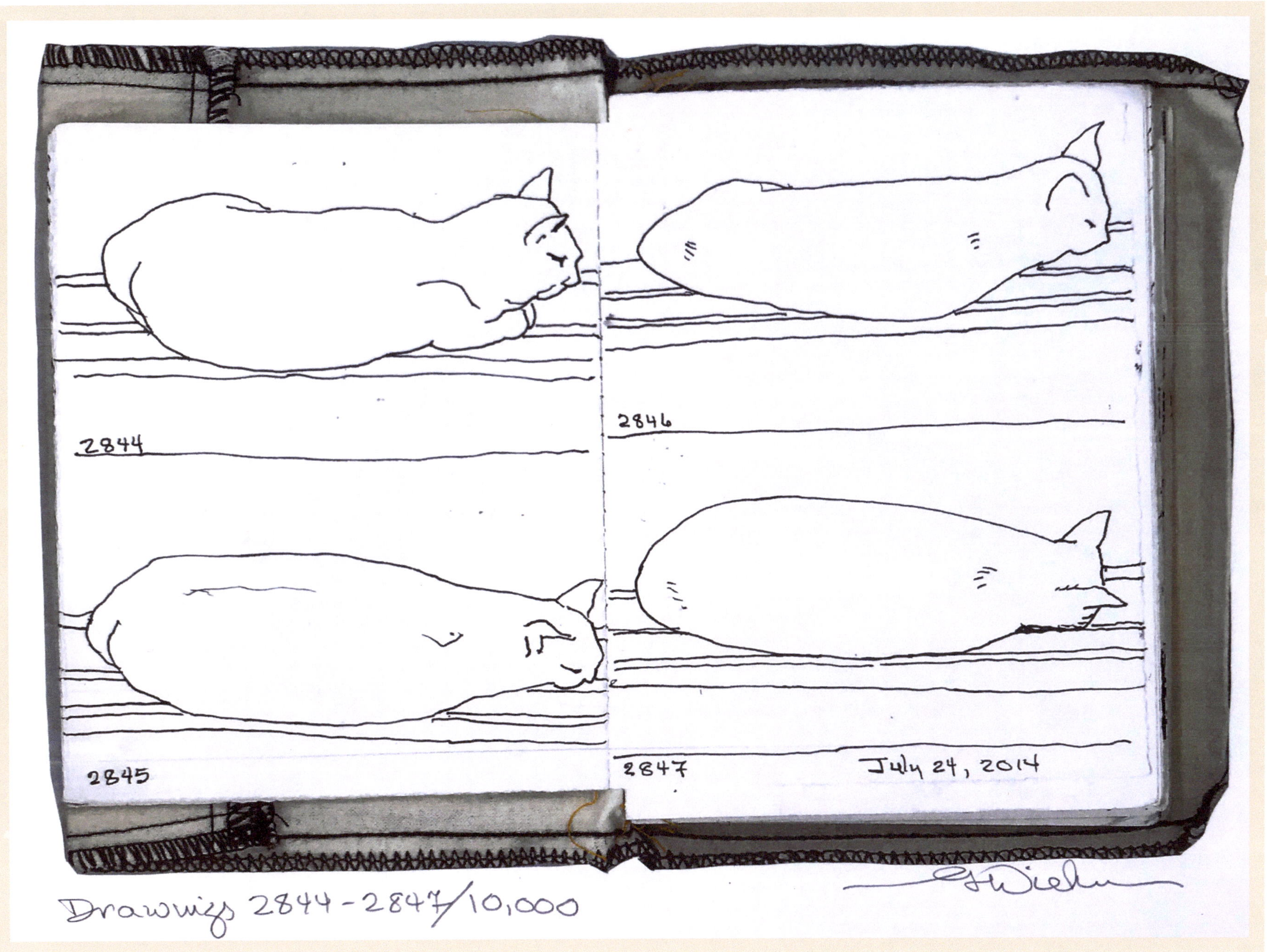

Drawings 2844 - 2847/10,000

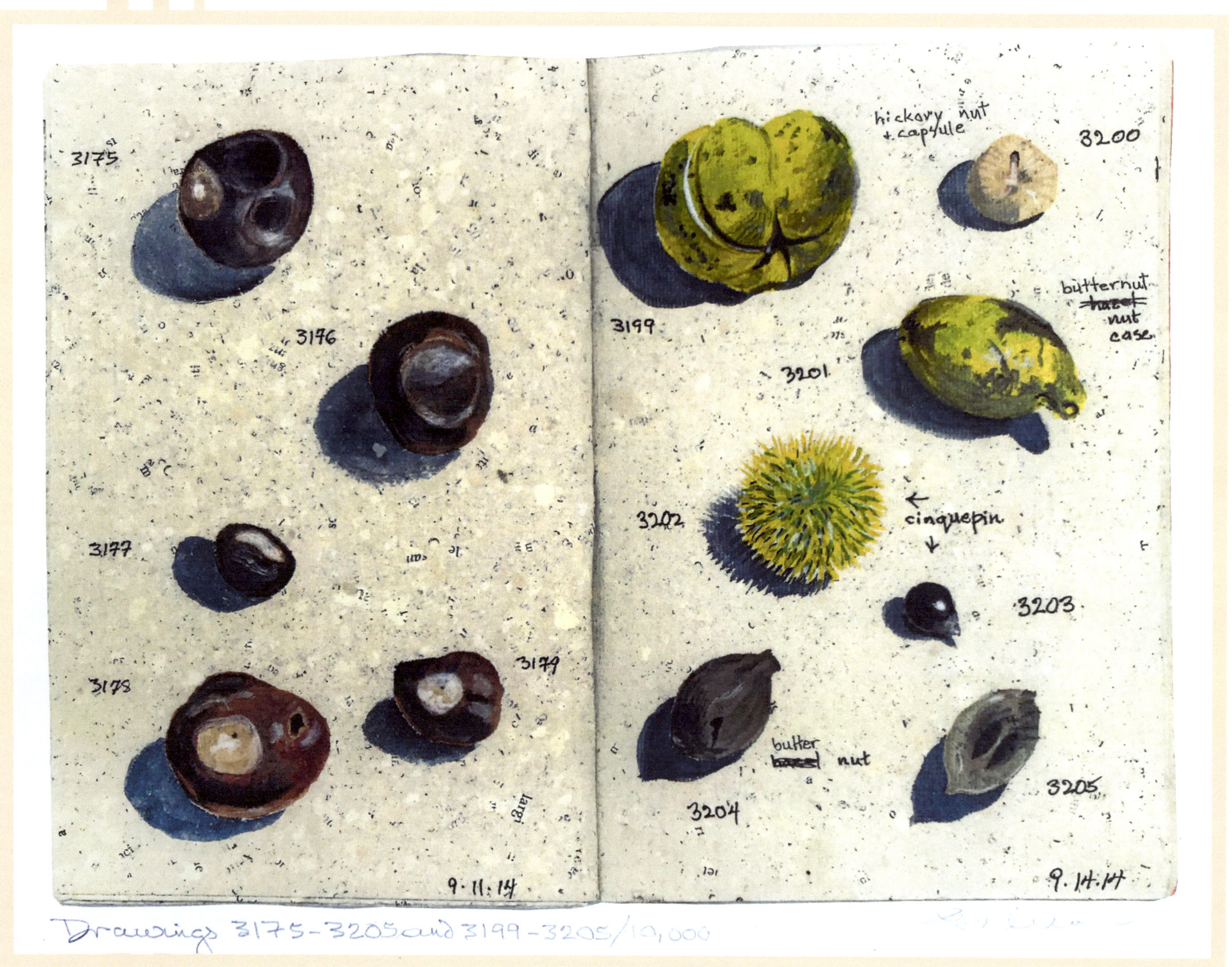

3175
3176
3177
3178
3179
9.11.14
hickory nut
+ capsule
3200
3199
butternut
hazel nut
case
3201
3202
cinquepin
3203
butter
hazel nut
3204
3205
9.14.14
Drawings 3175-3205 and 3199-3205/10,000

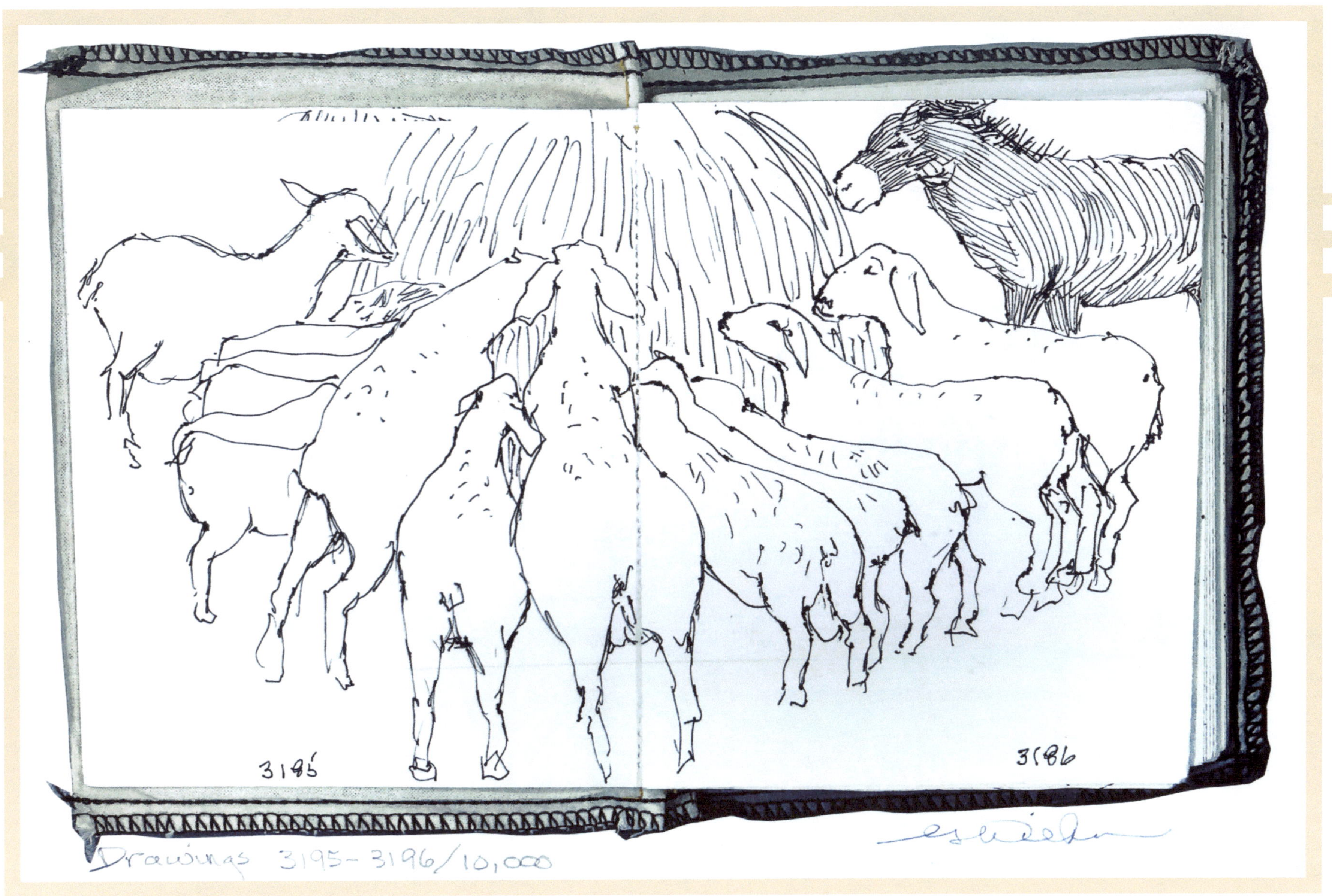
3195
3196
Drawings 3195-3196/10,000

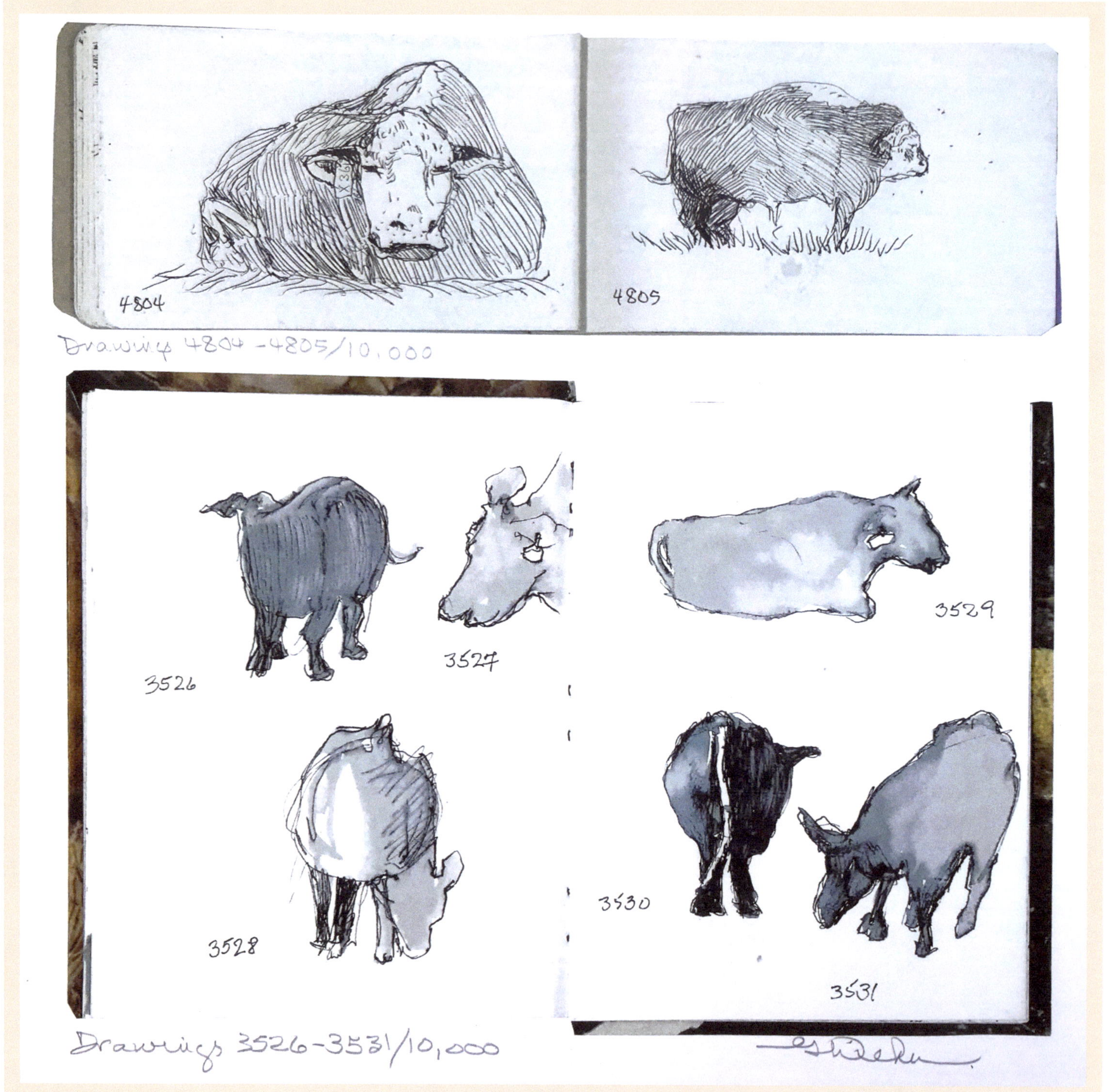

4804
4805
3526
3527
3528
3529
3530
3531
Drawing 4804 - 4805/10,000
Drawings 3526 - 3531/10,000

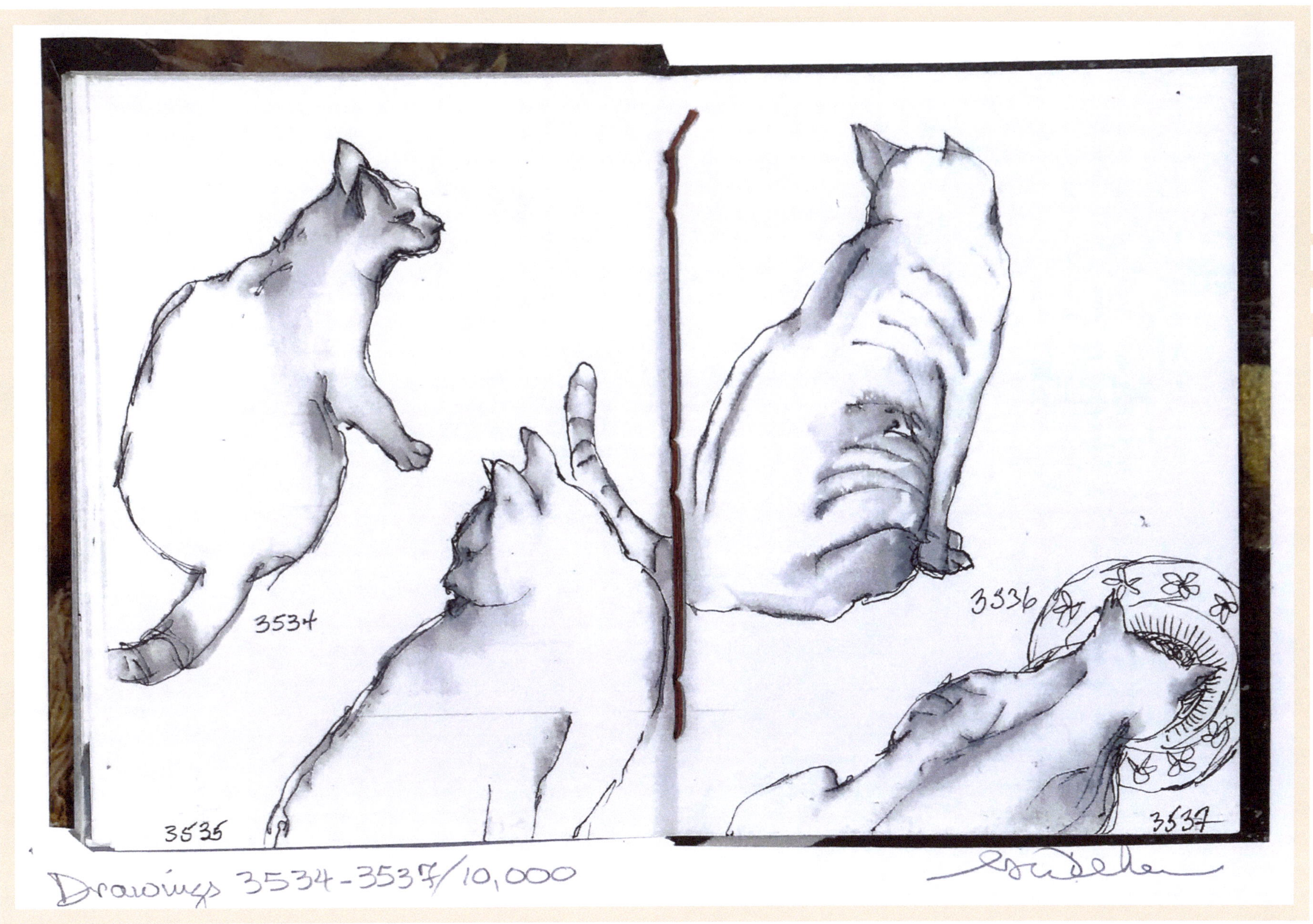

3534
3535
3536
3537
Drawings 3534-3537/10,000

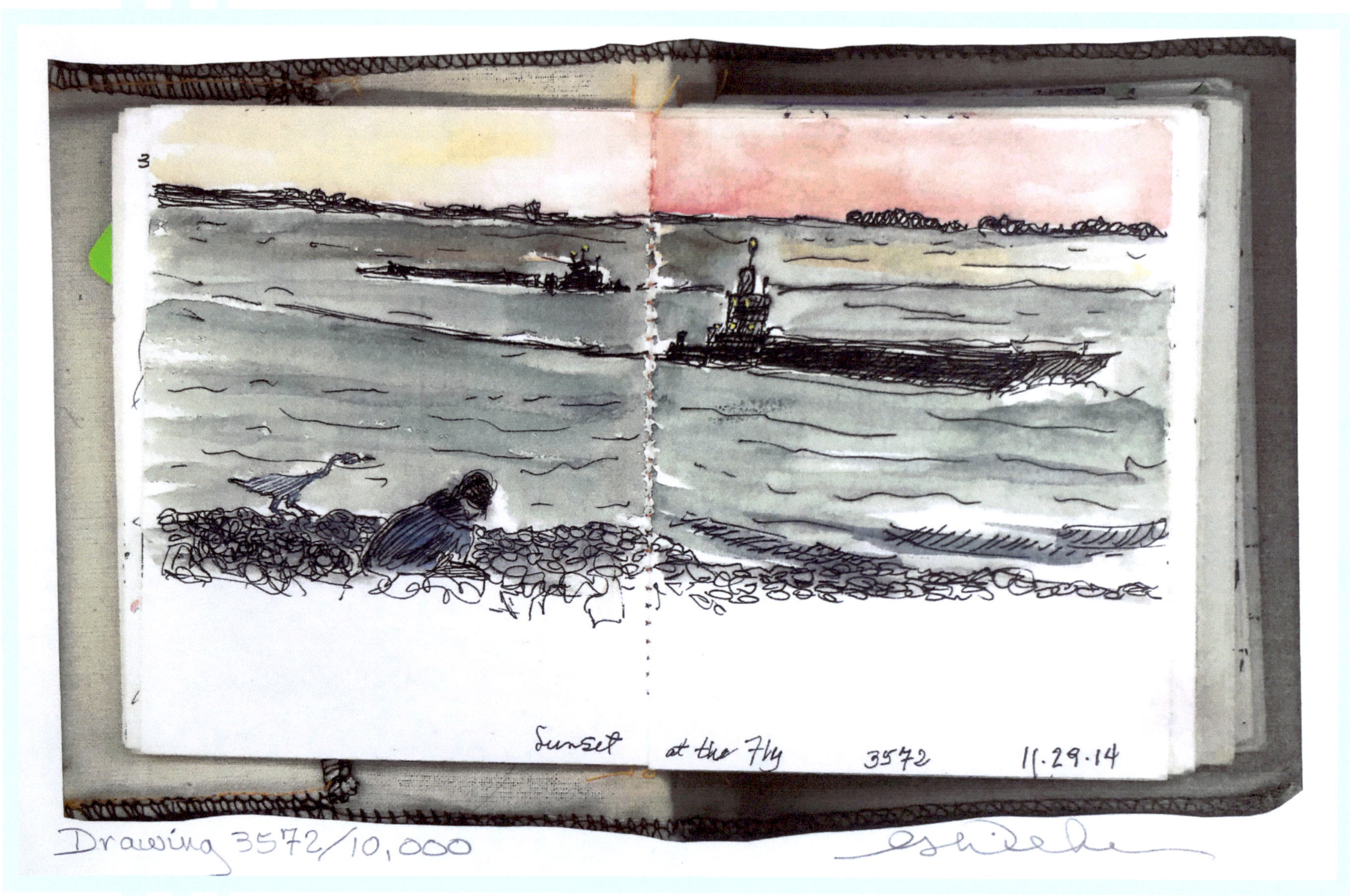

Sunset at the Fly   3572   11·29·14
Drawing 3572/10,000

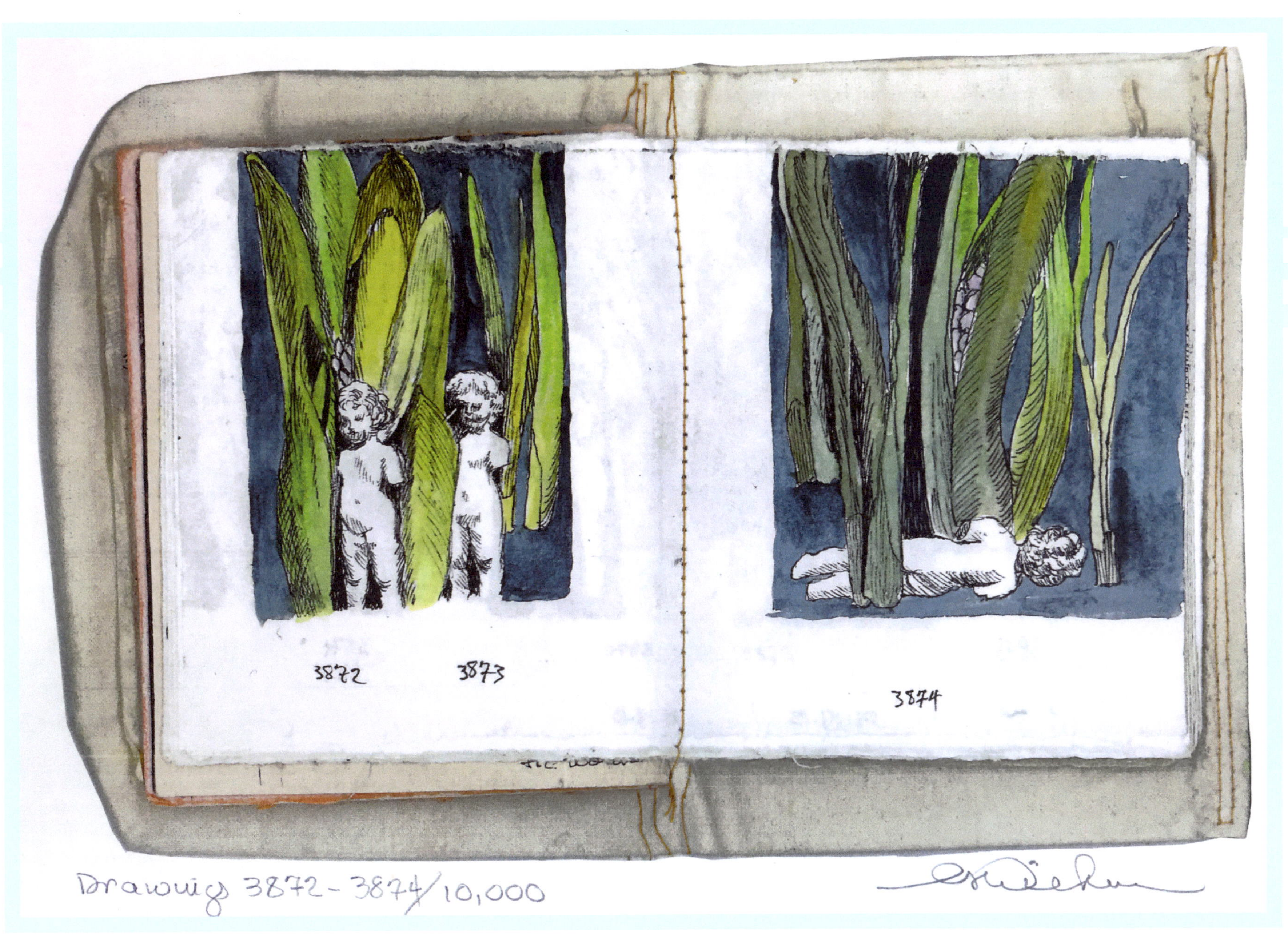

Drawing 3872 - 3874 / 10,000

21

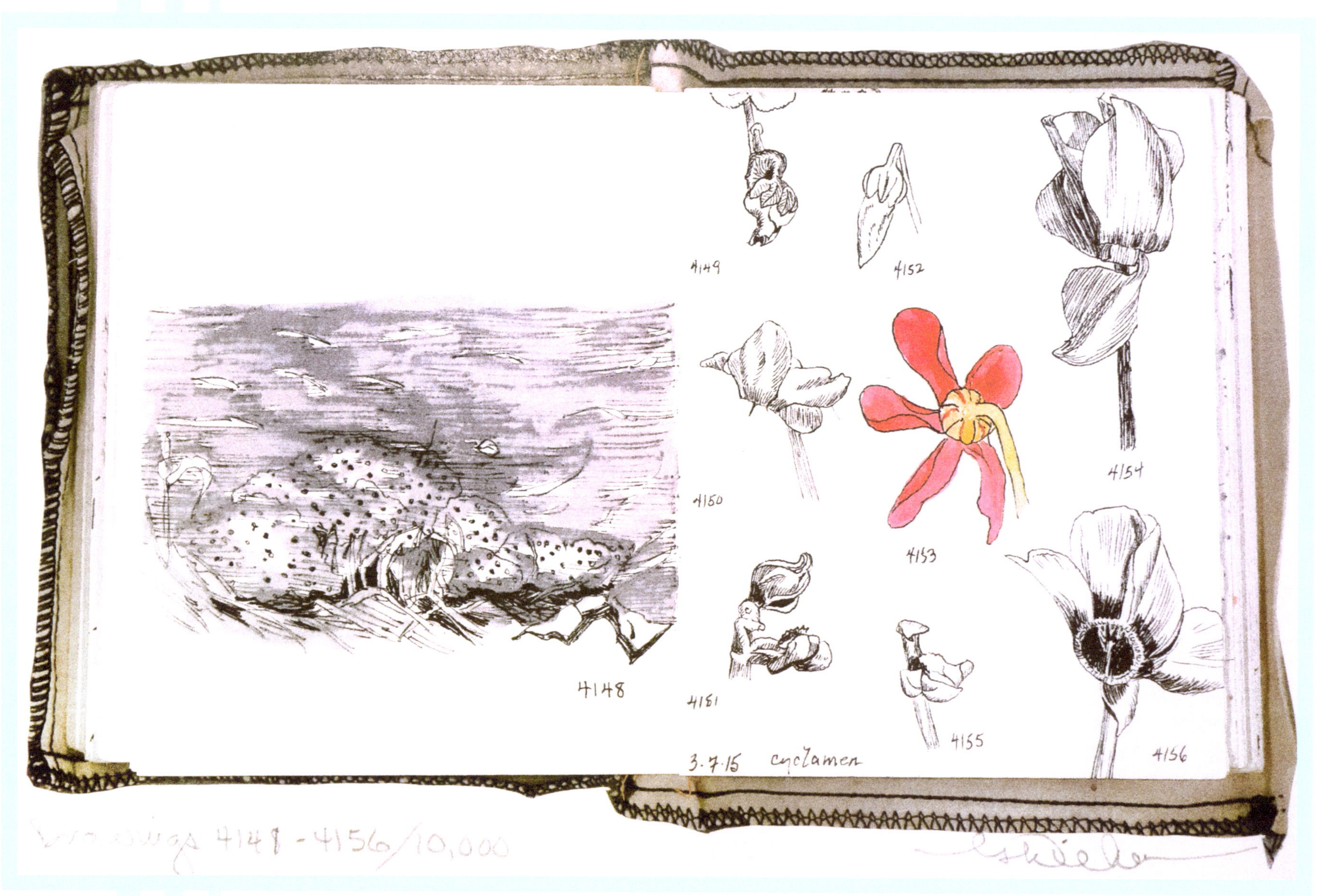

4149
4152
4150
4153
4154
4148
4151
4155
4156
3.7.15   cyclamen

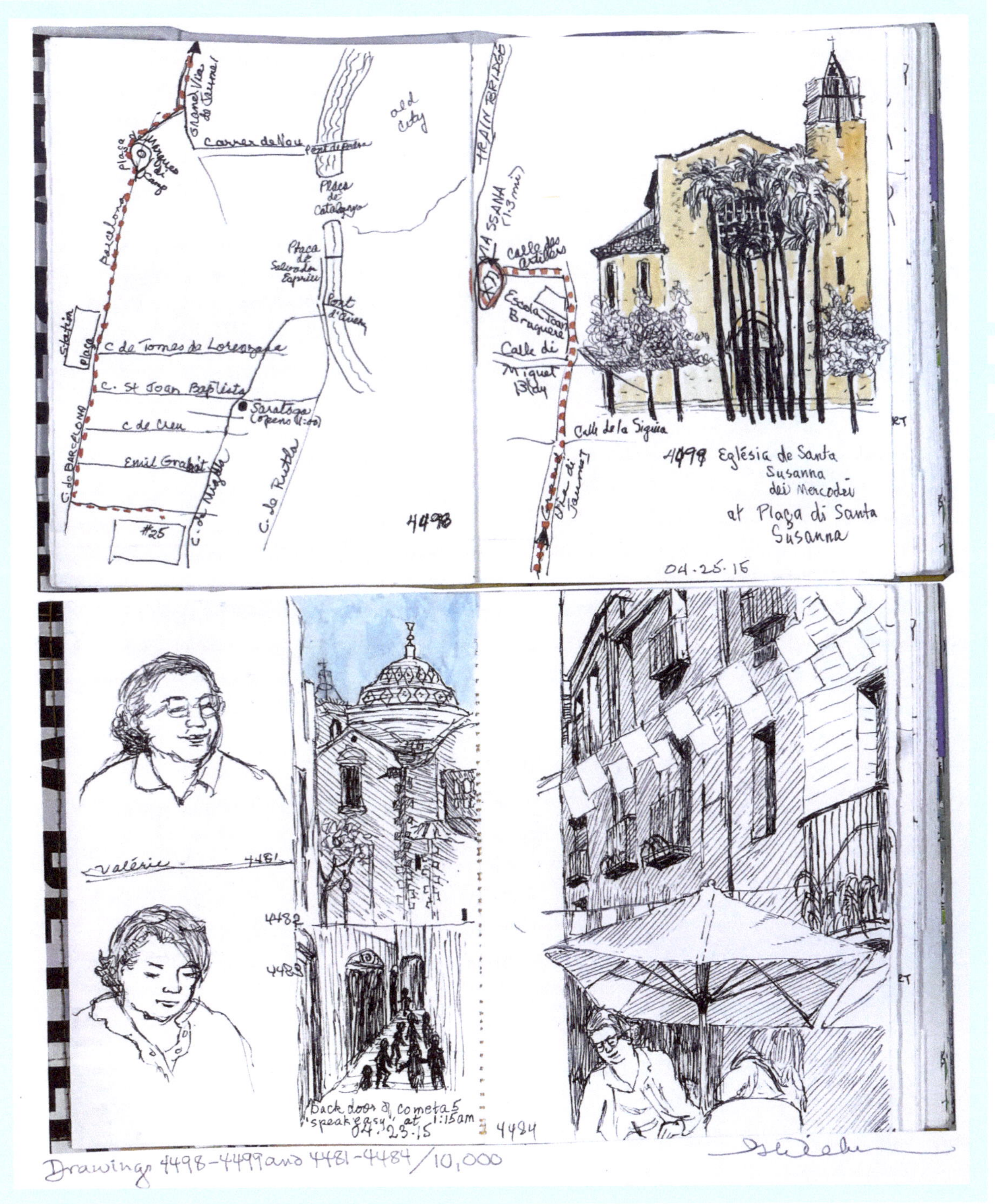

4498

4499 Eglésia de Santa Susanna dei Mercedei at Plaça di Santa Susanna

04·25·15

Valérie 4481

4482

4483

Back door of cometa5 "speakeasy" at 1:15am 04·25·15 4484

Drawings 4498–4499 and 4481–4484 / 10,000

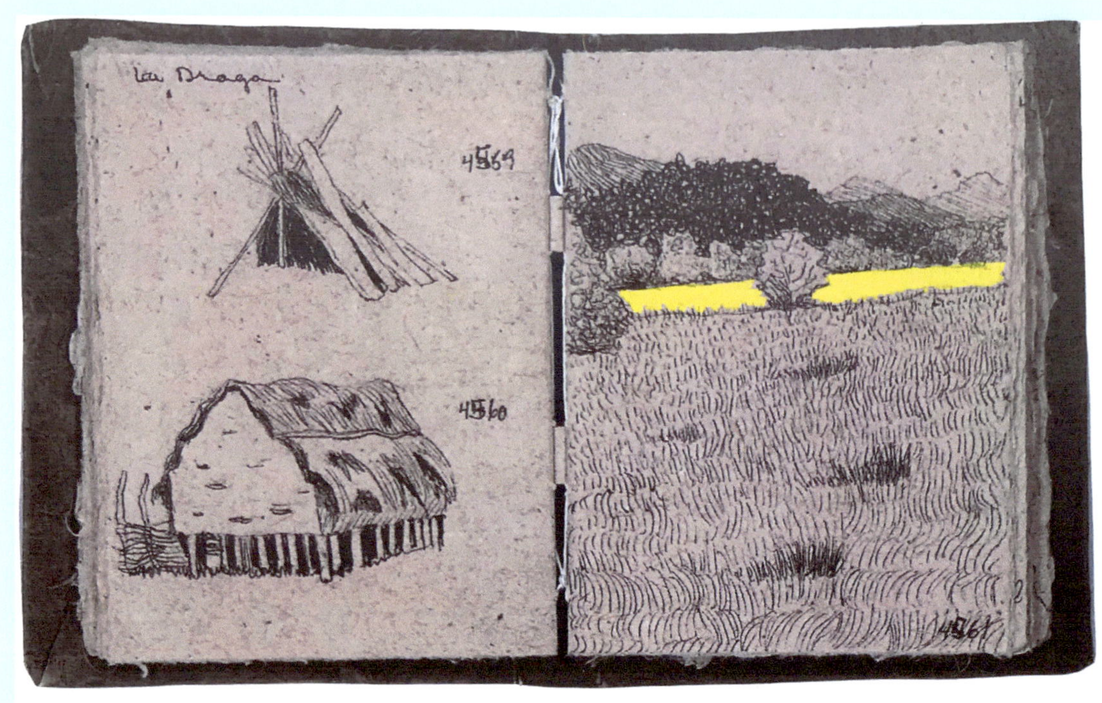

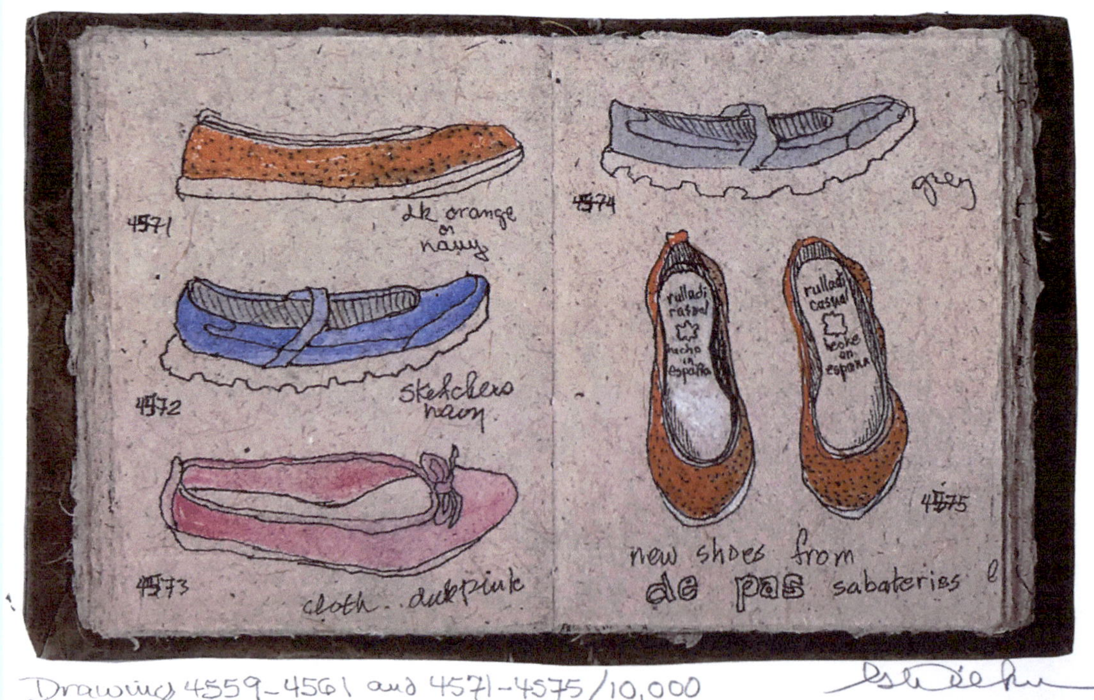

Drawing 4559-4561 and 4571-4575/10,000

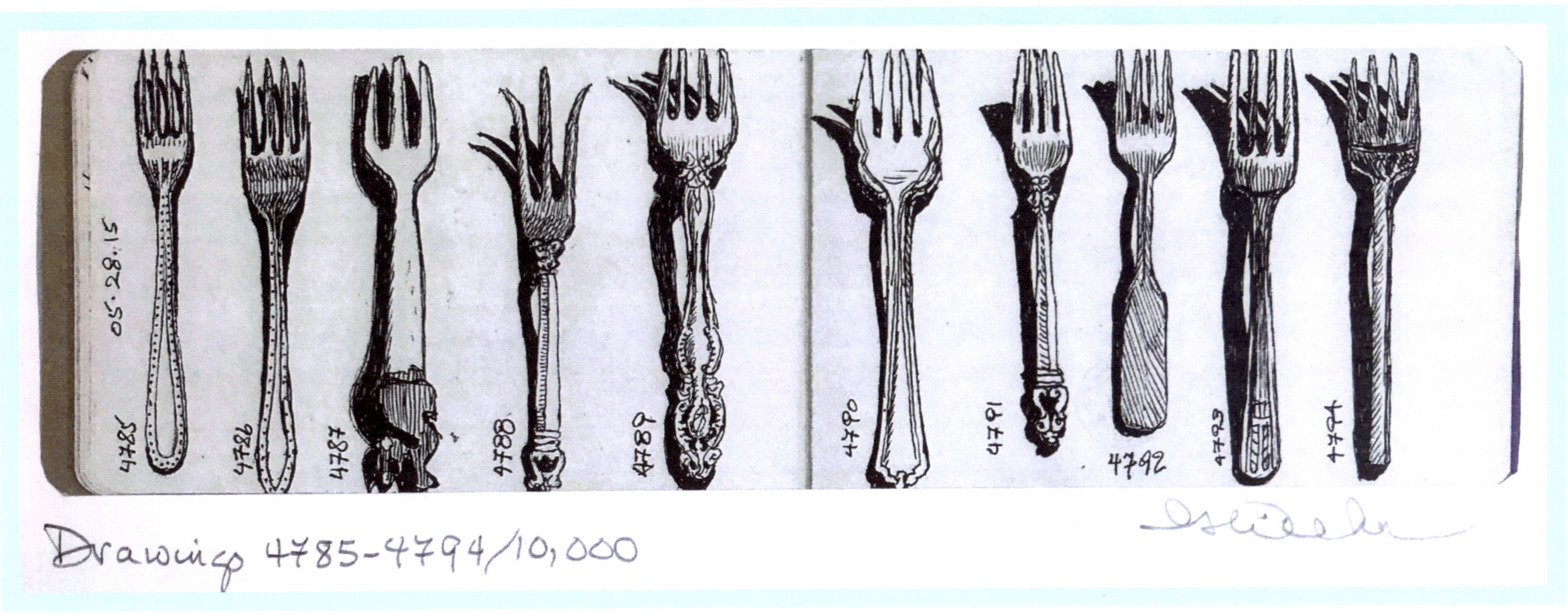

Drawings 4785-4794/10,000

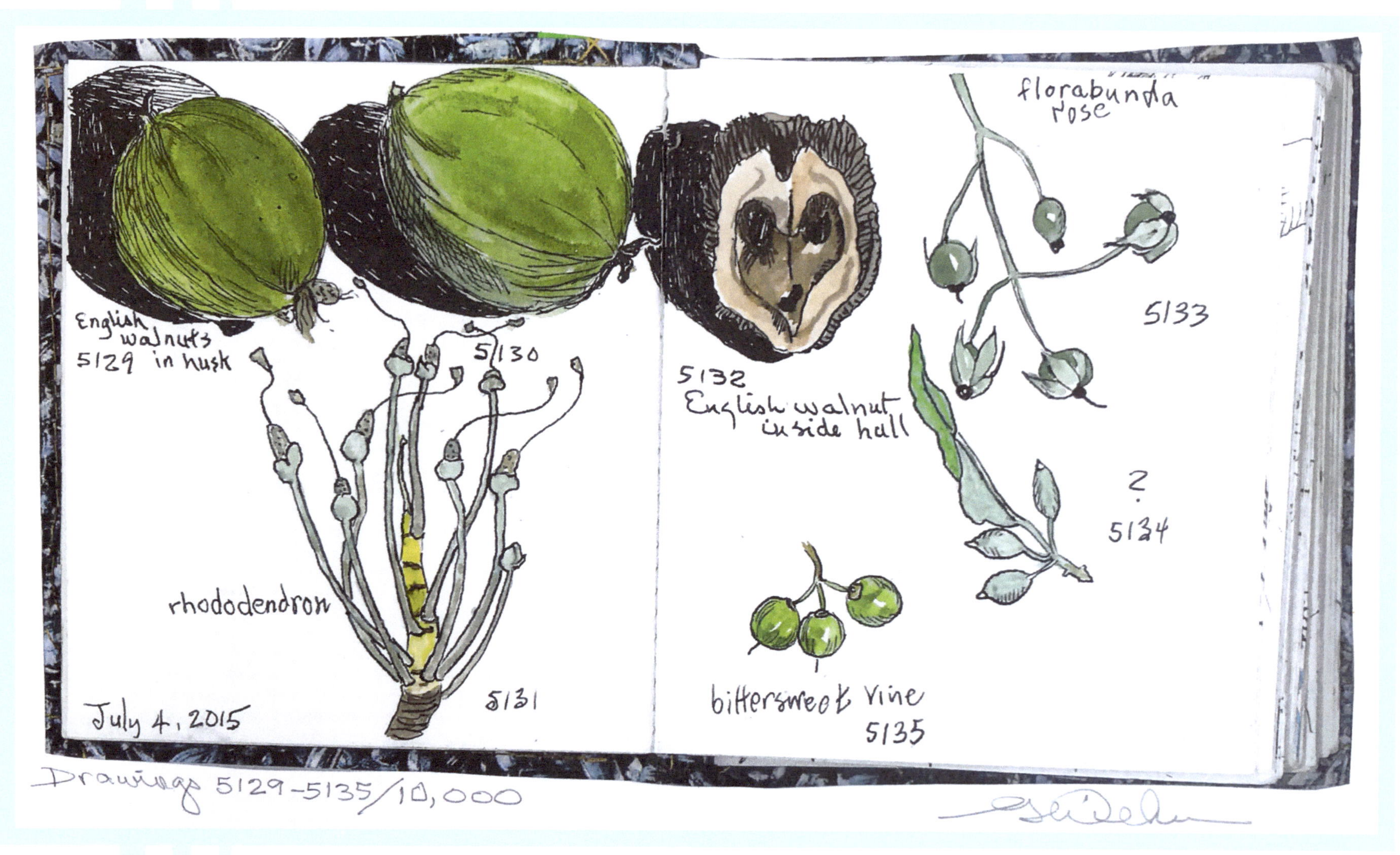

florabunda rose
English walnuts 5129 in husk
5130
5131
rhododendron
July 4, 2015
5132 English walnut inside hull
5133
2. 5134
bittersweet vine 5135
Drawings 5129-5135/10,000

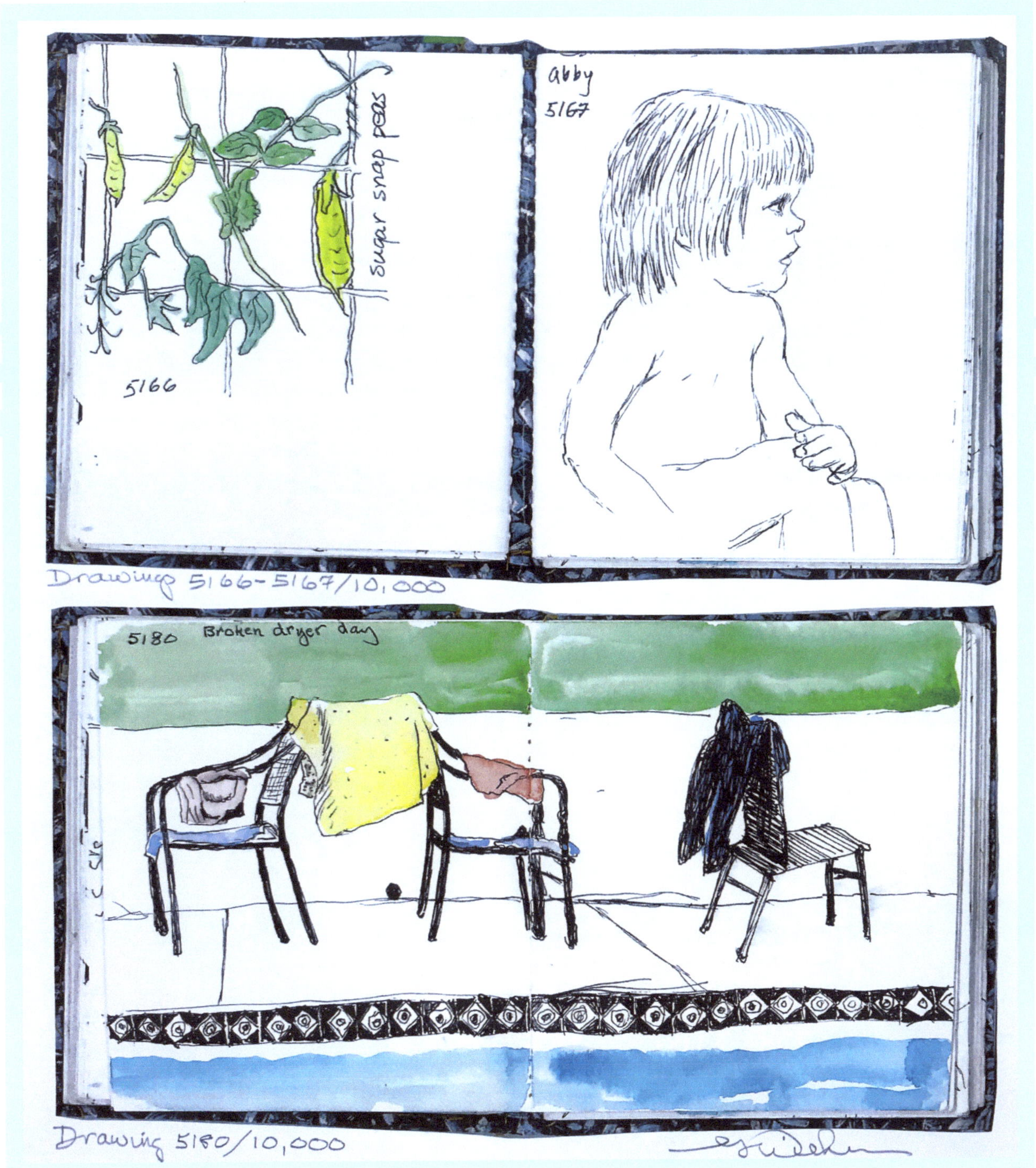

sugar snap peas
5166
abby
5167
Drawing 5166-5167/10,000
5180 Broken dryer day
Drawing 5180/10,000

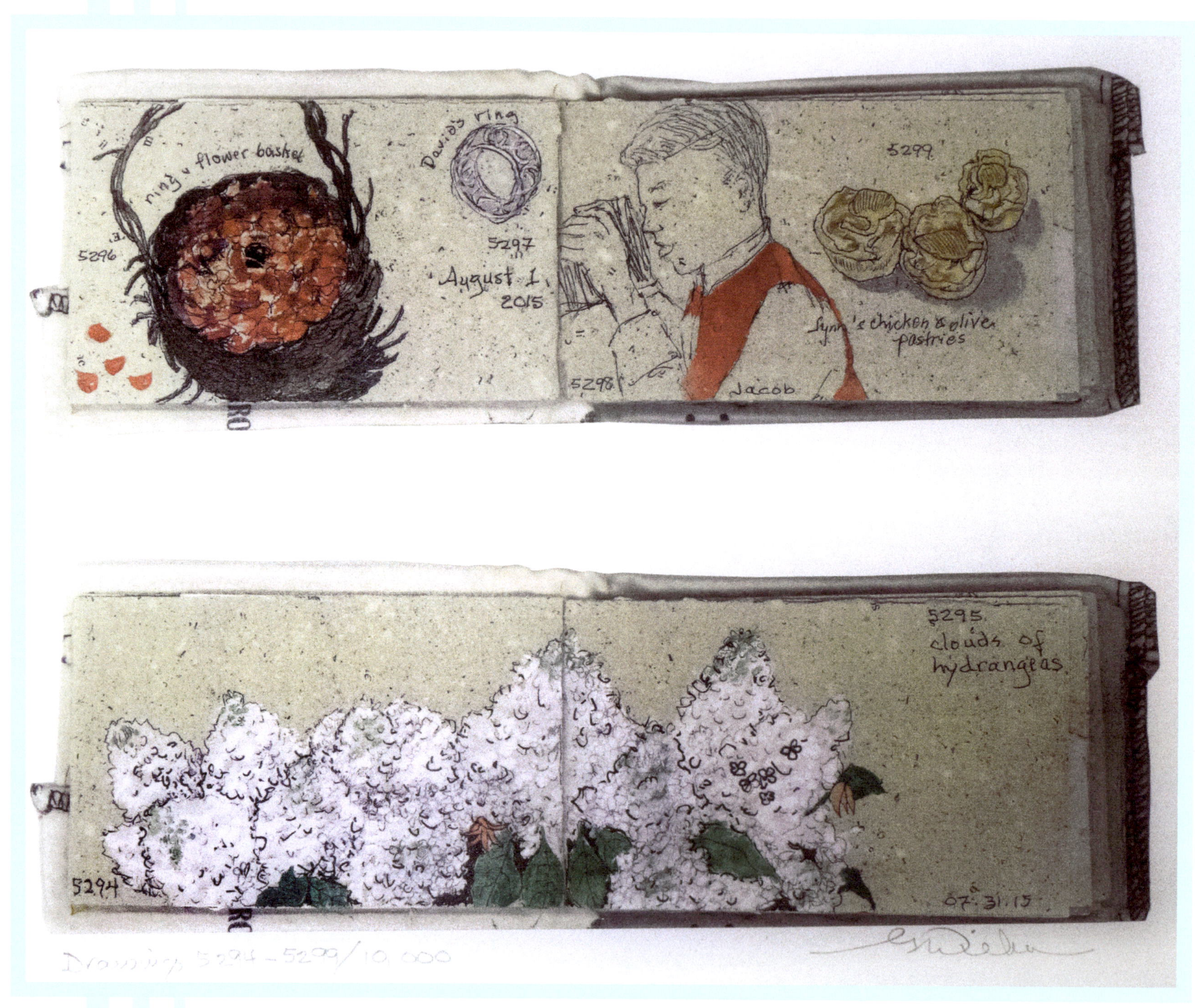

ring ~ flower basket
David's ring
5299
5297
August 1, 2015
5296
Lynn's chicken & olive pastries
5298
Jacob
5295.
clouds of hydrangeas
5294
07·31·15
Drawing 5294 - 5299 / 10,000

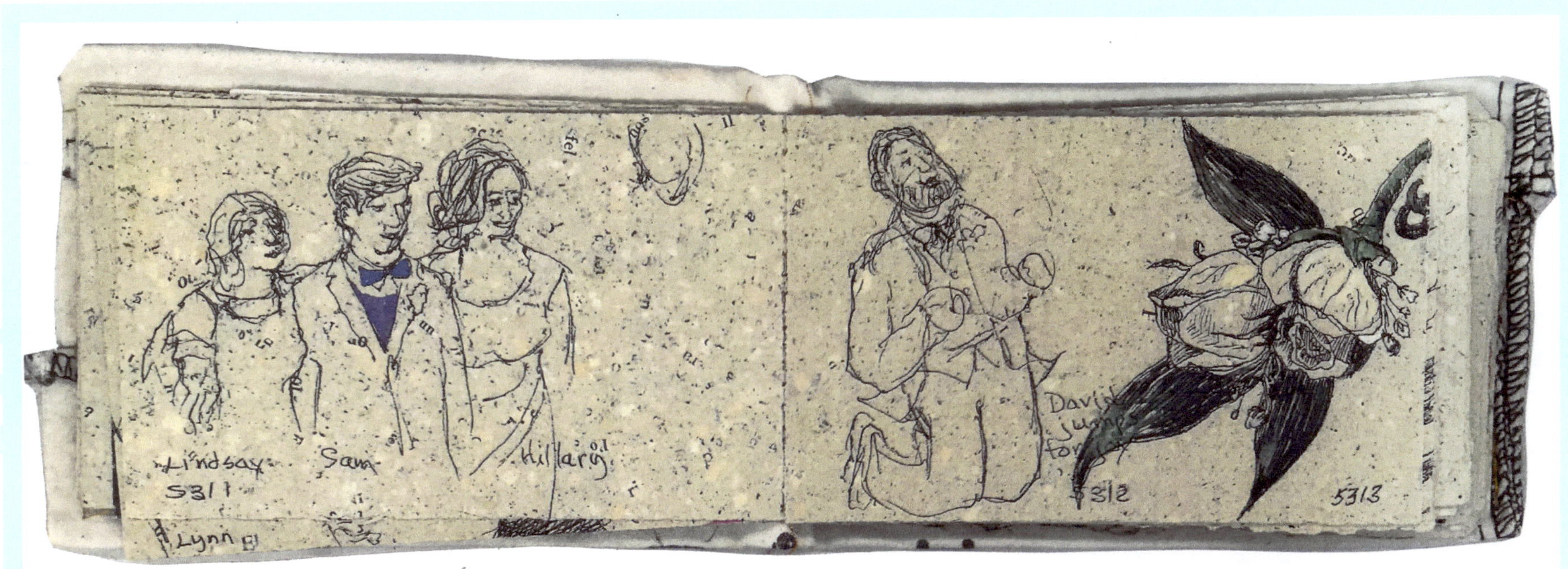

Drawings 5311-5313/10,000

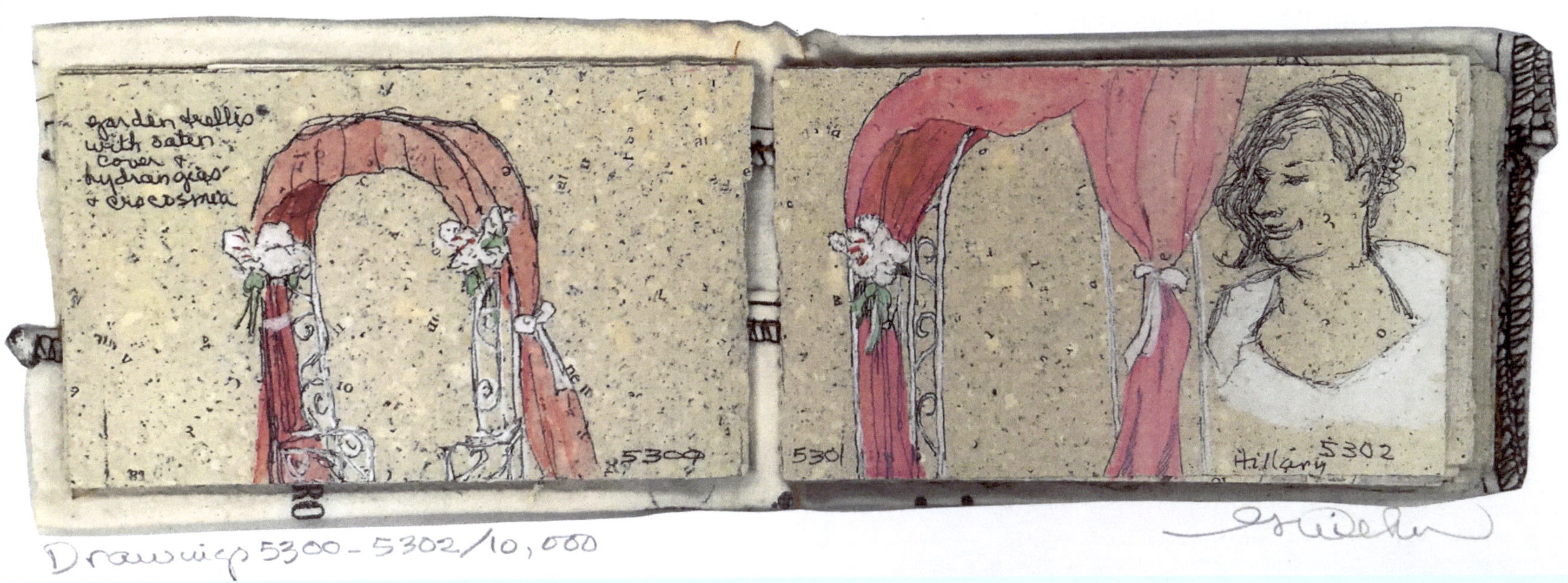

Drawings 5300-5302/10,000

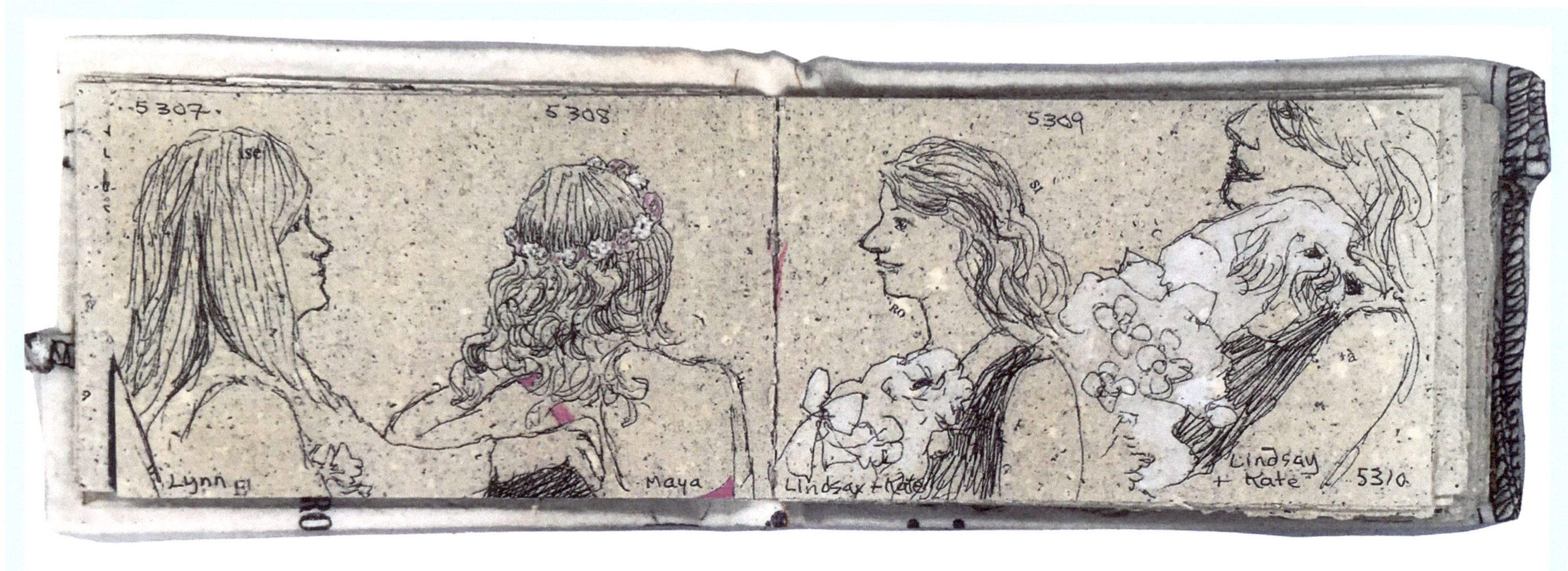

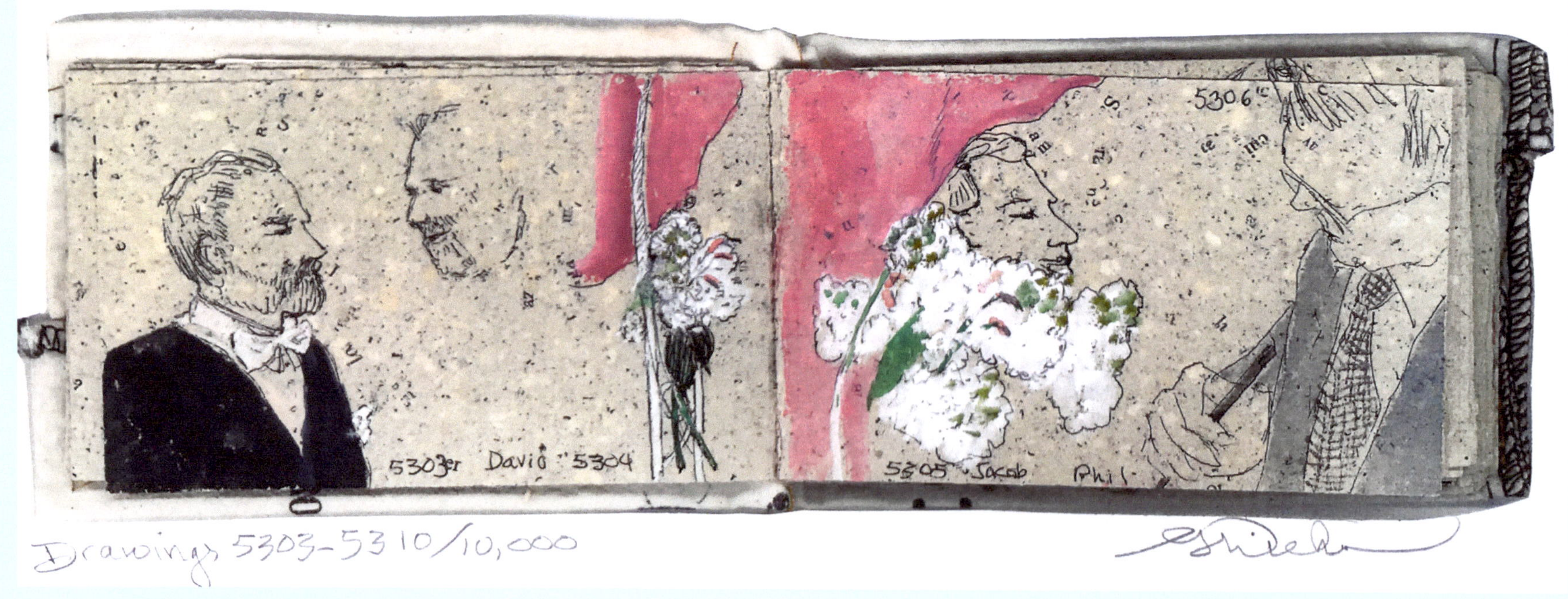

Drawings 5303-5310/10,000

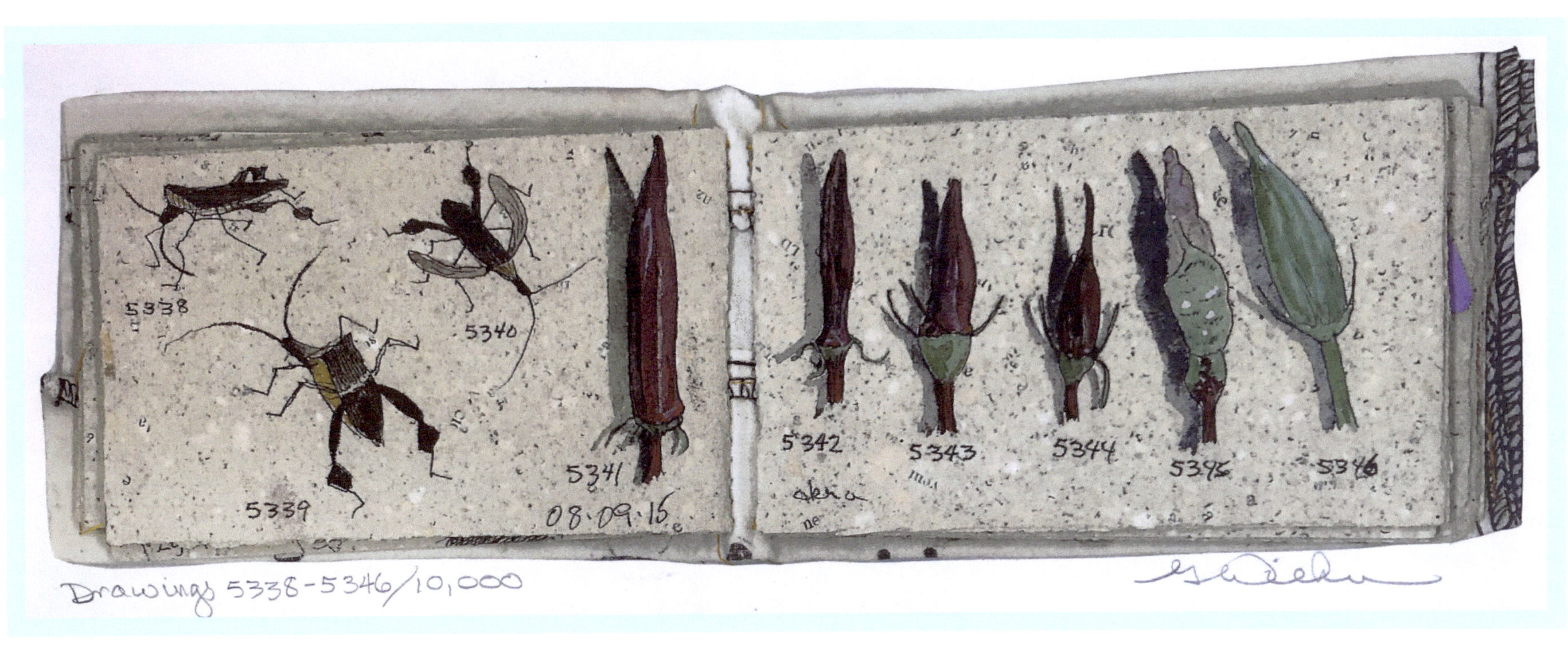

Drawings 5338-5346/10,000

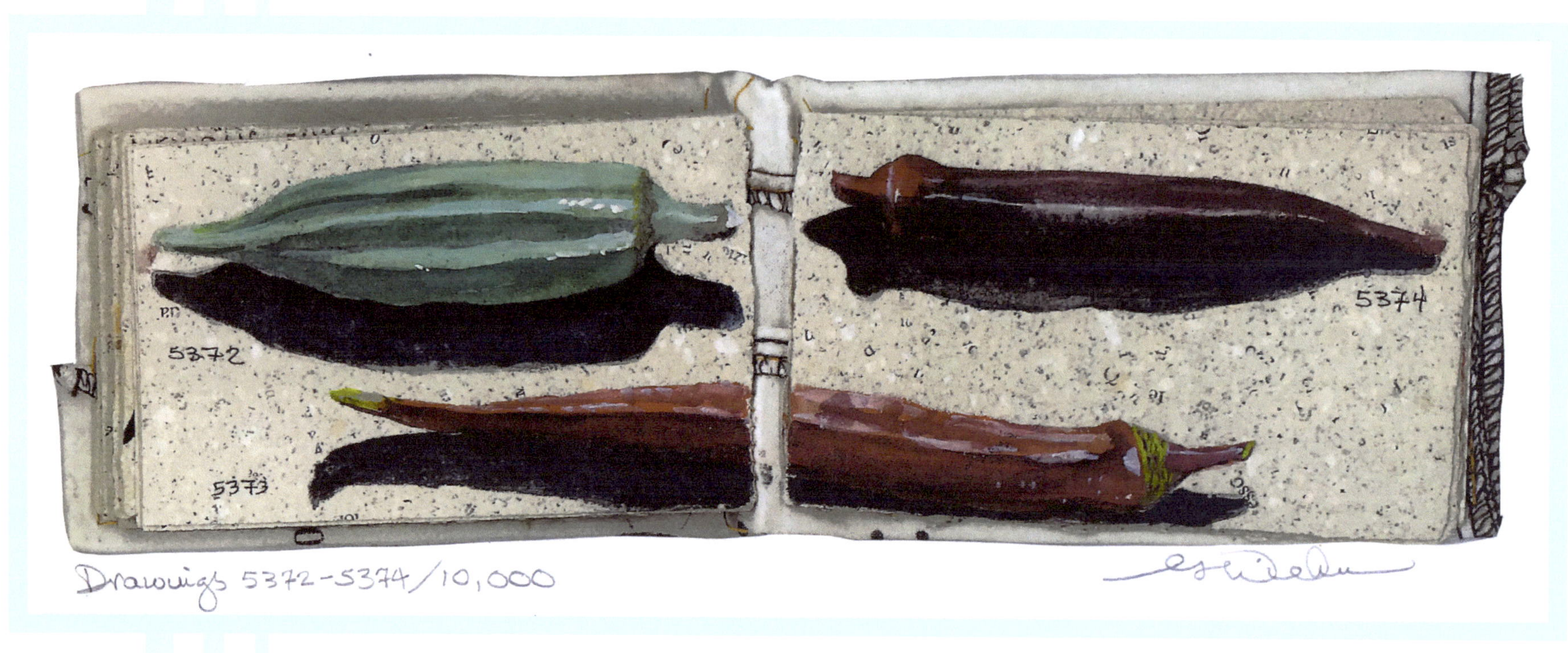

Drawings 5372-5374/10,000

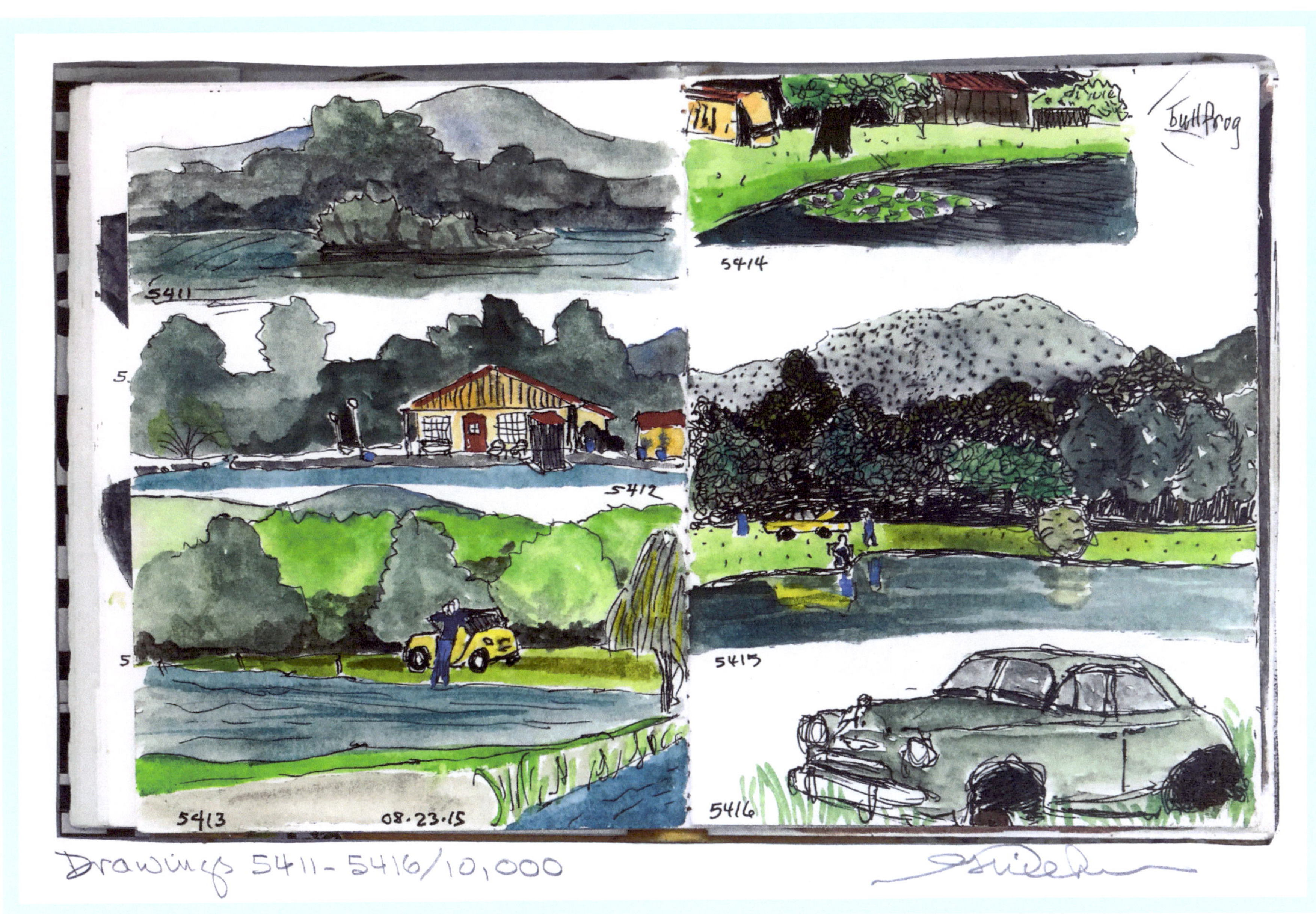

bullfrog
5411
5414
5412
5413
08·23·15
5415
5416
Drawings 5411 - 5416/10,000

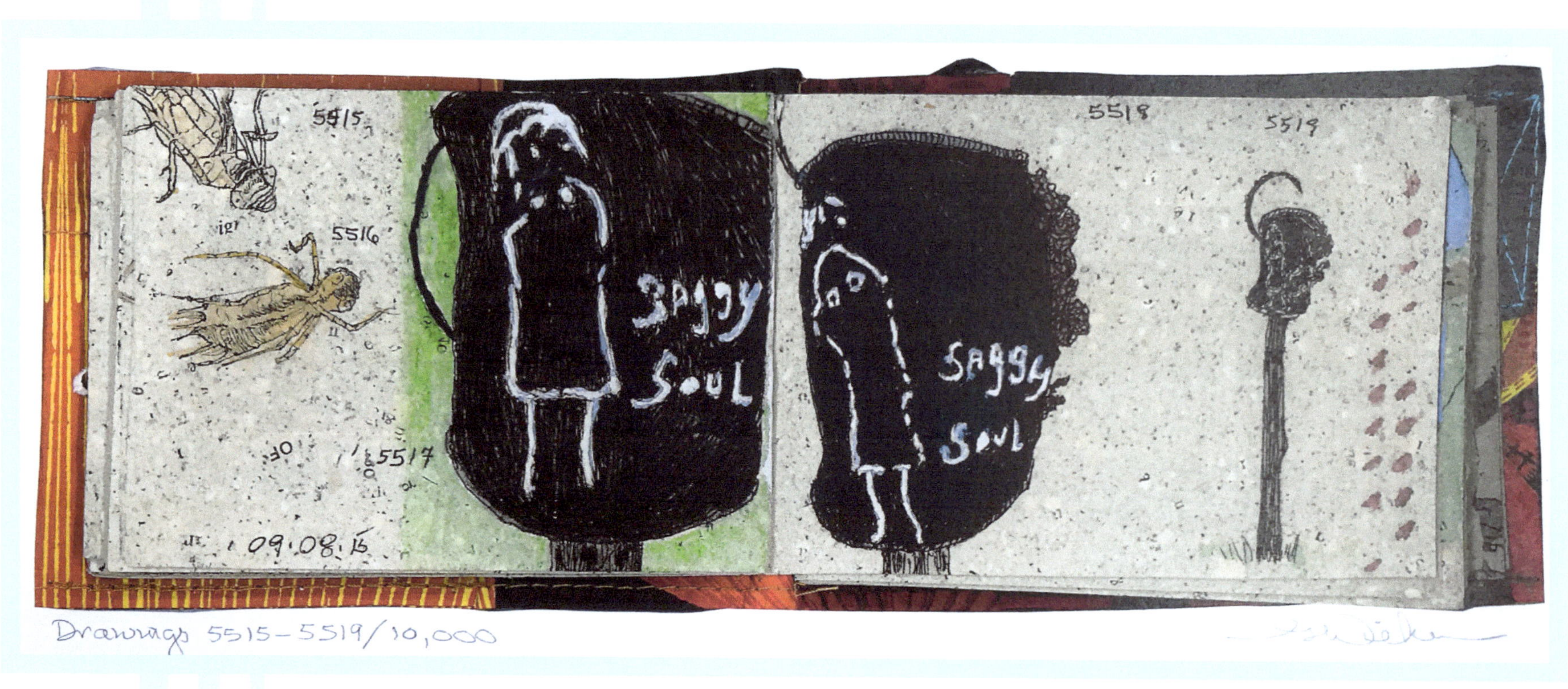

Drawings 5515–5519/10,000

34

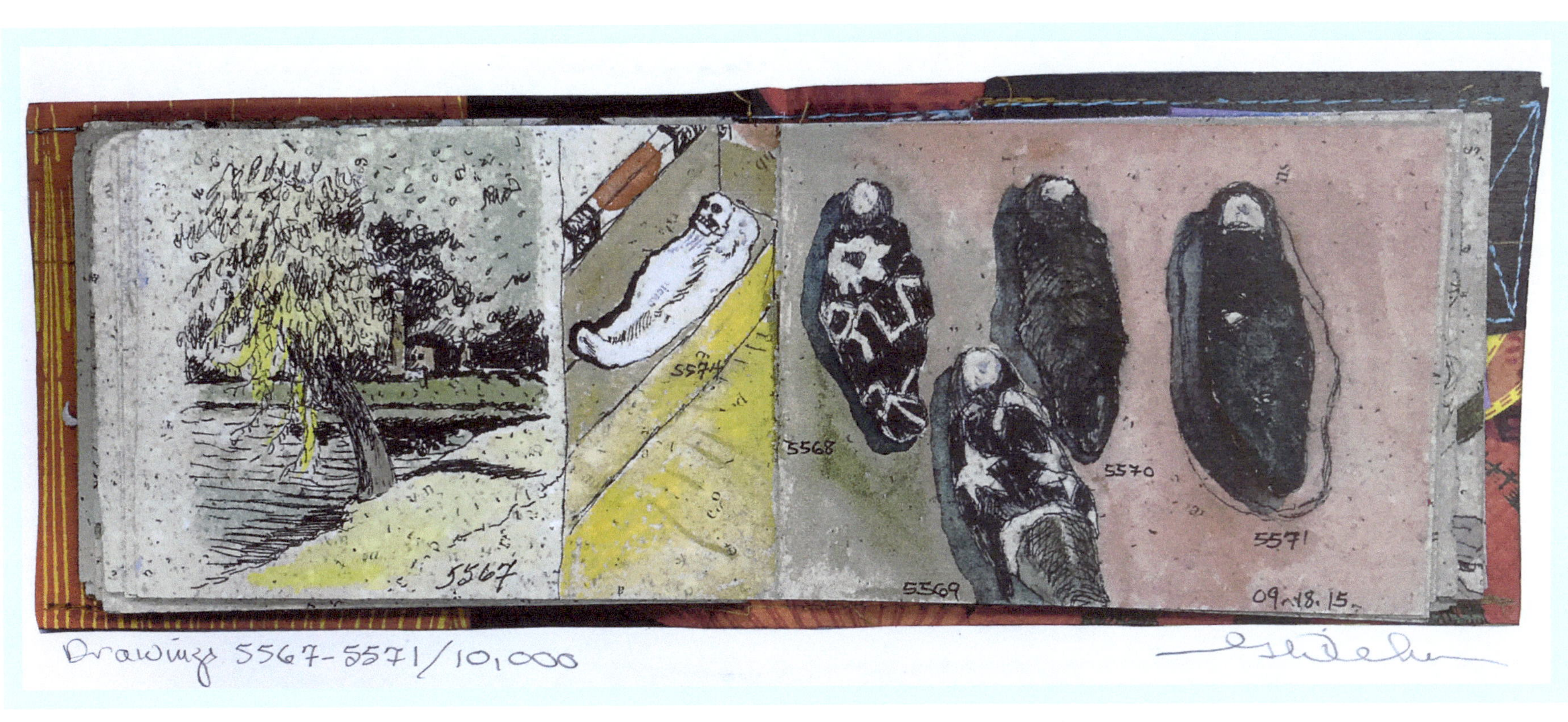

Drawings 5567-5571/10,000

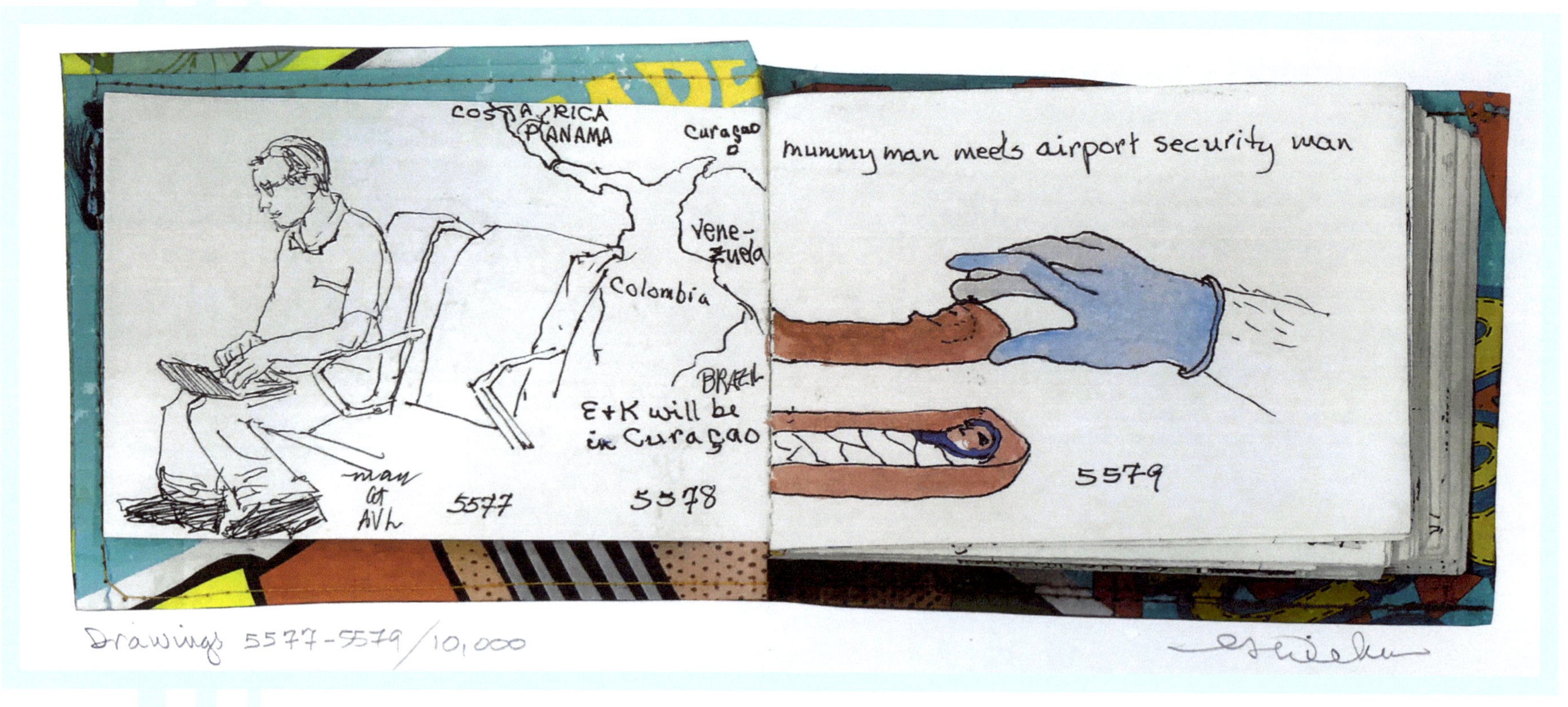

Drawings 5577-5579/10,000

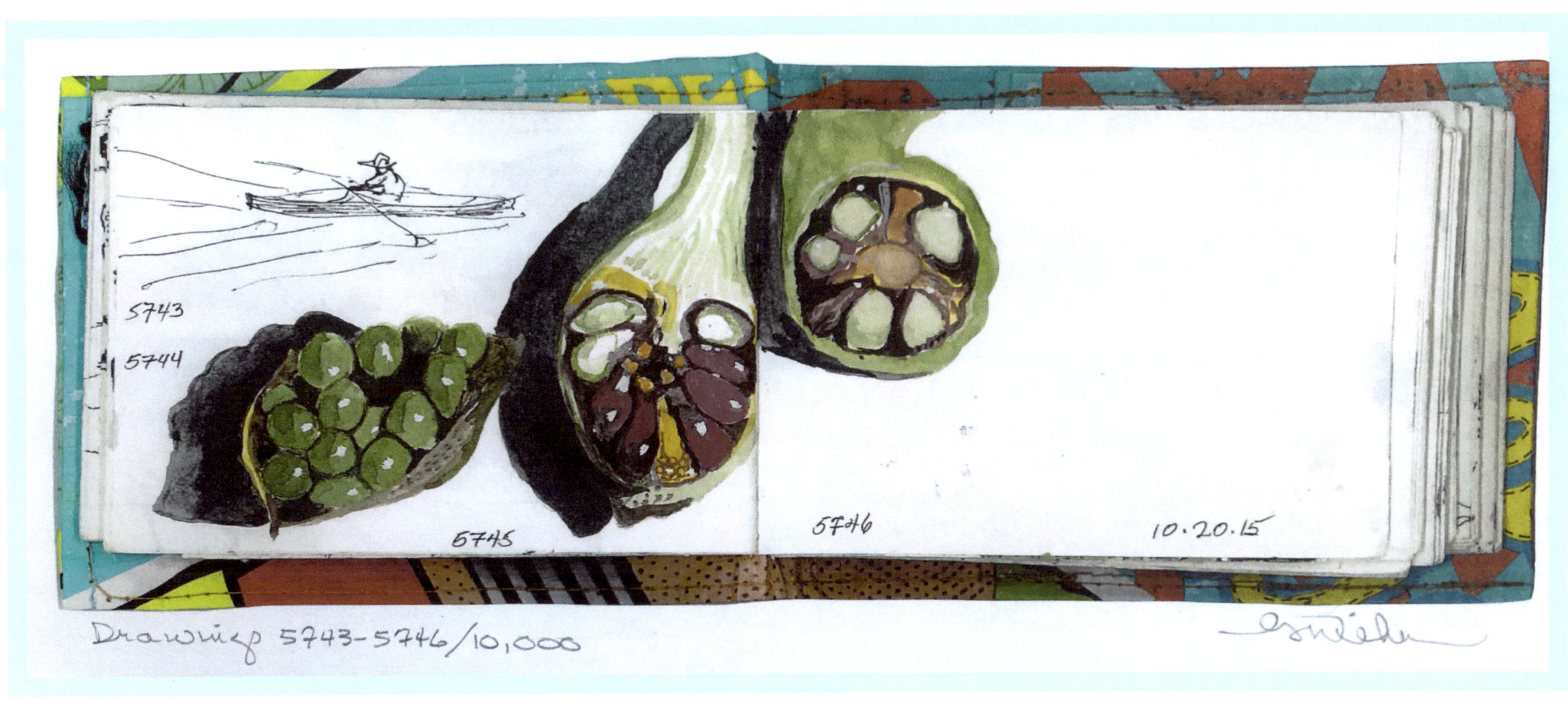

5743
5744
5745
5746
10.20.15
Drawing 5743-5746/10,000

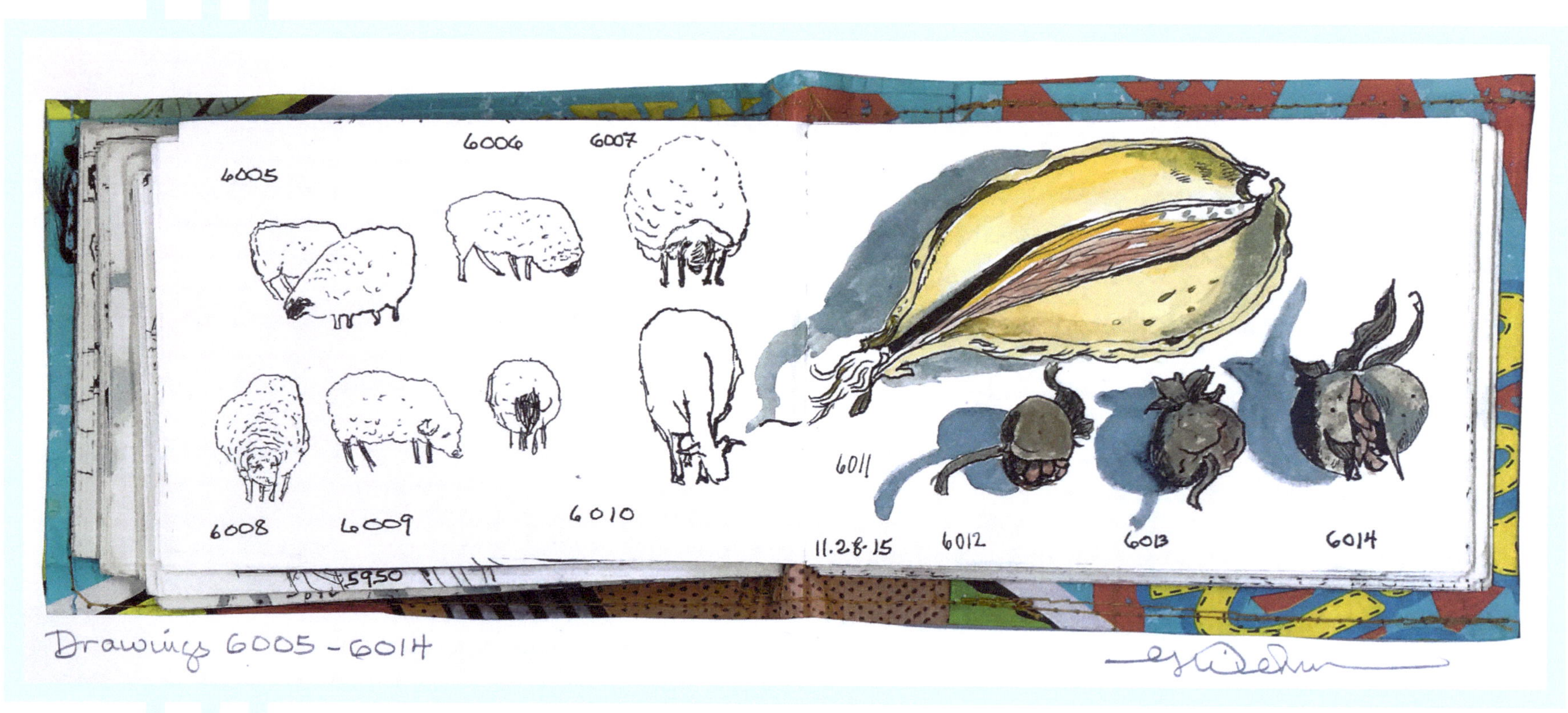

Drawings 6005 - 6014

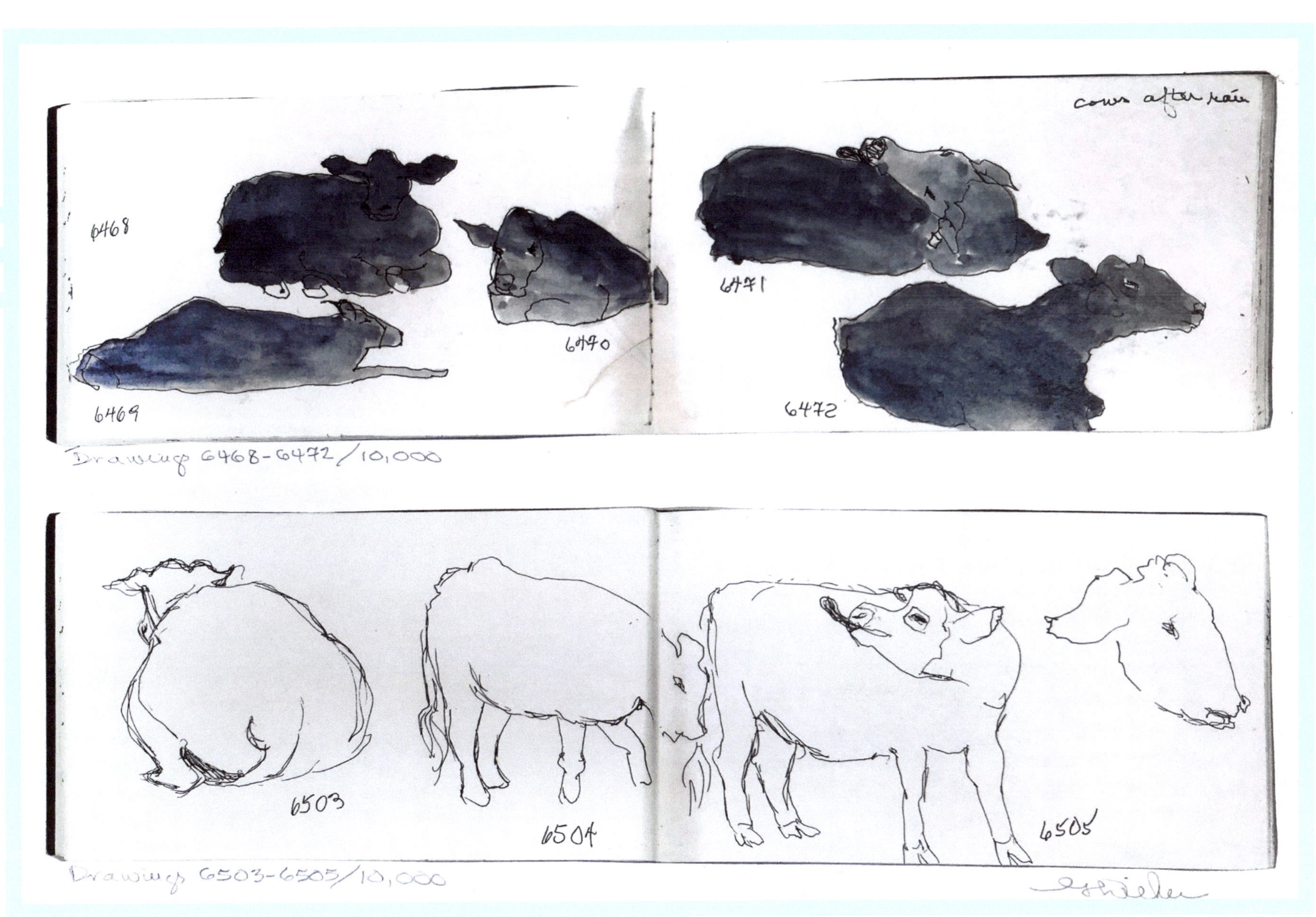

cows after rain
6468
6469
6470
6471
6472
Drawing 6468-6472/10,000
6503
6504
6505
Drawing 6503-6505/10,000

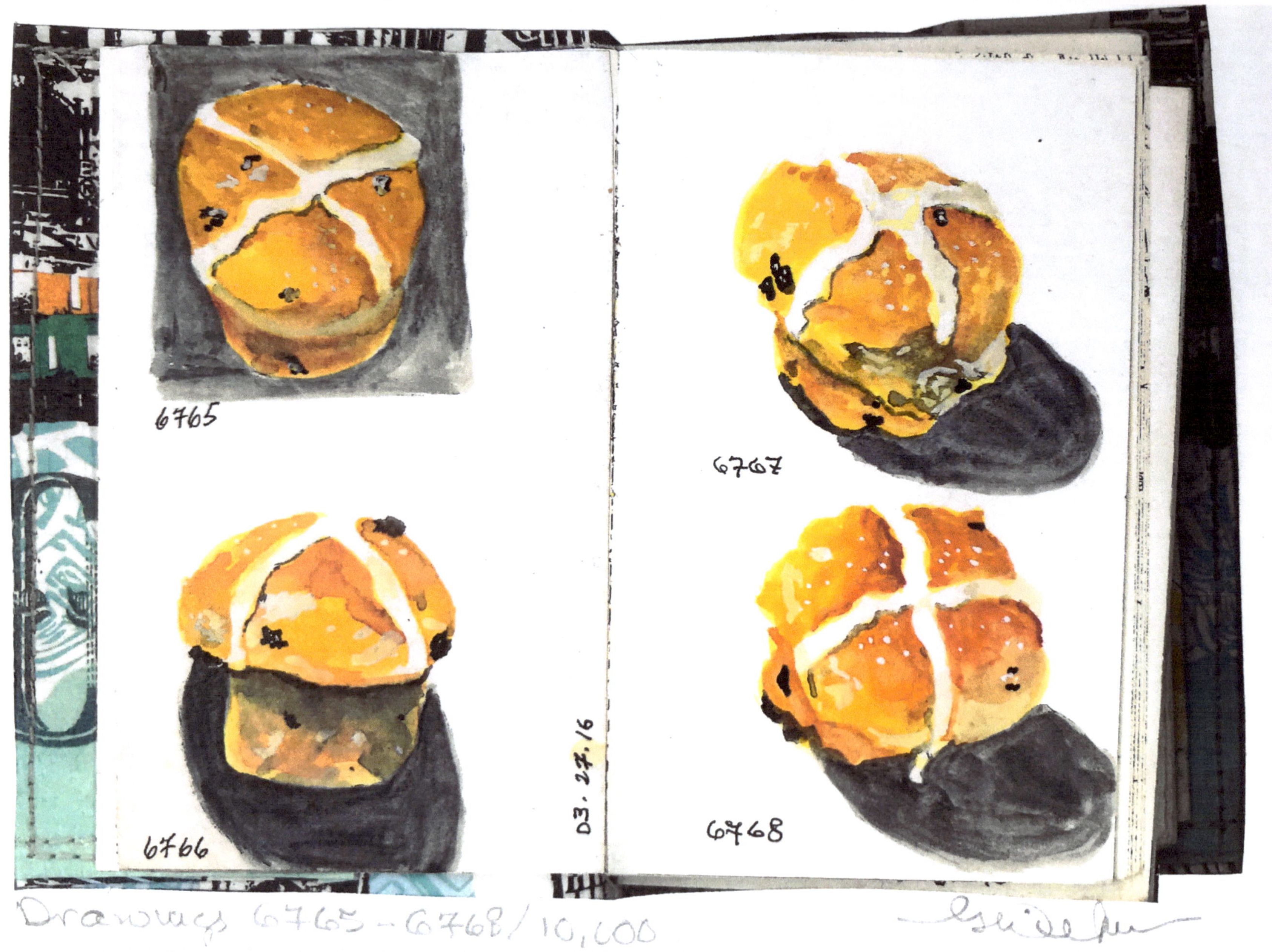

Drawings 6765 - 6768 / 10,000

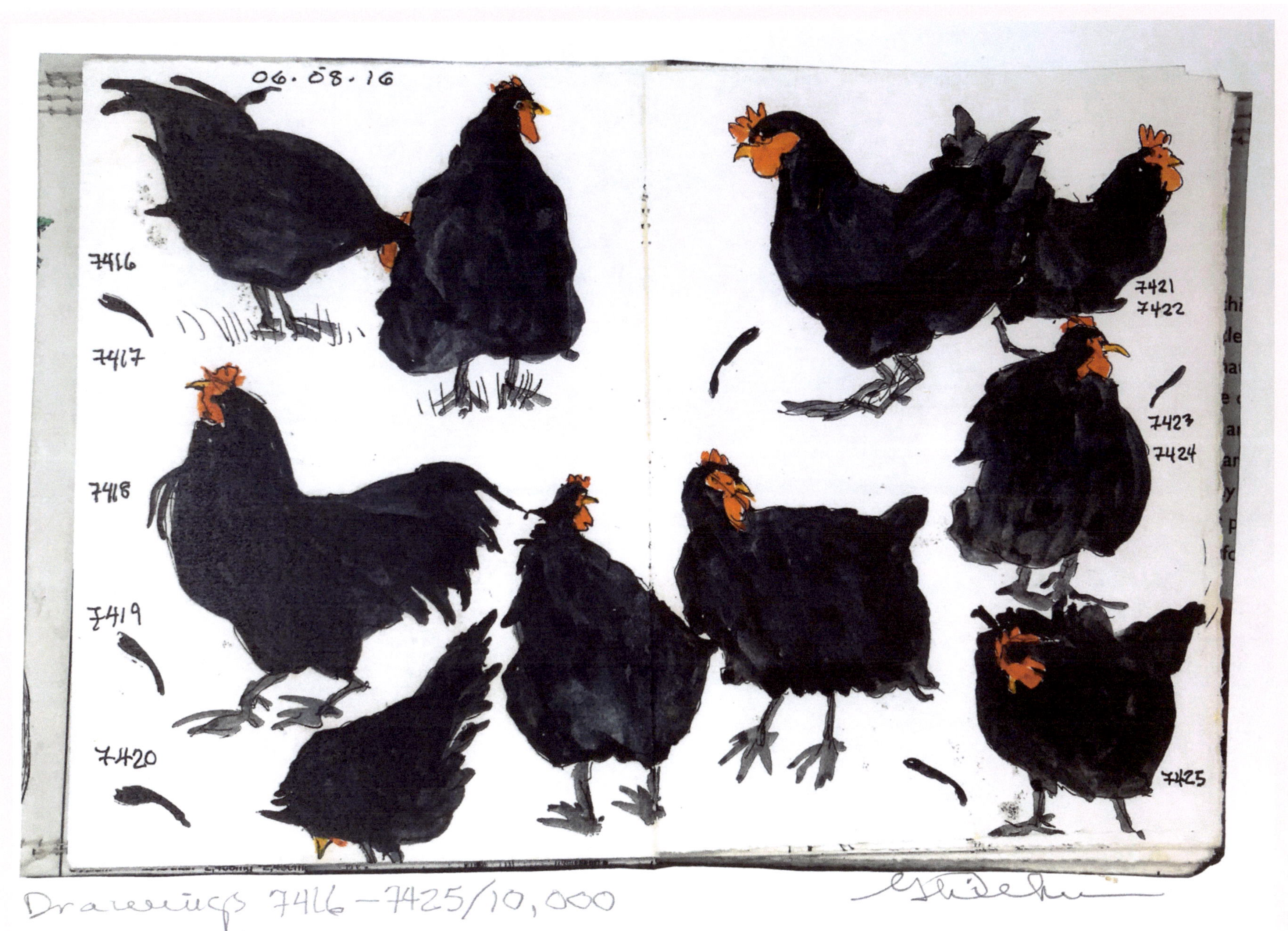

Drawings 7416 – 7425/10,000

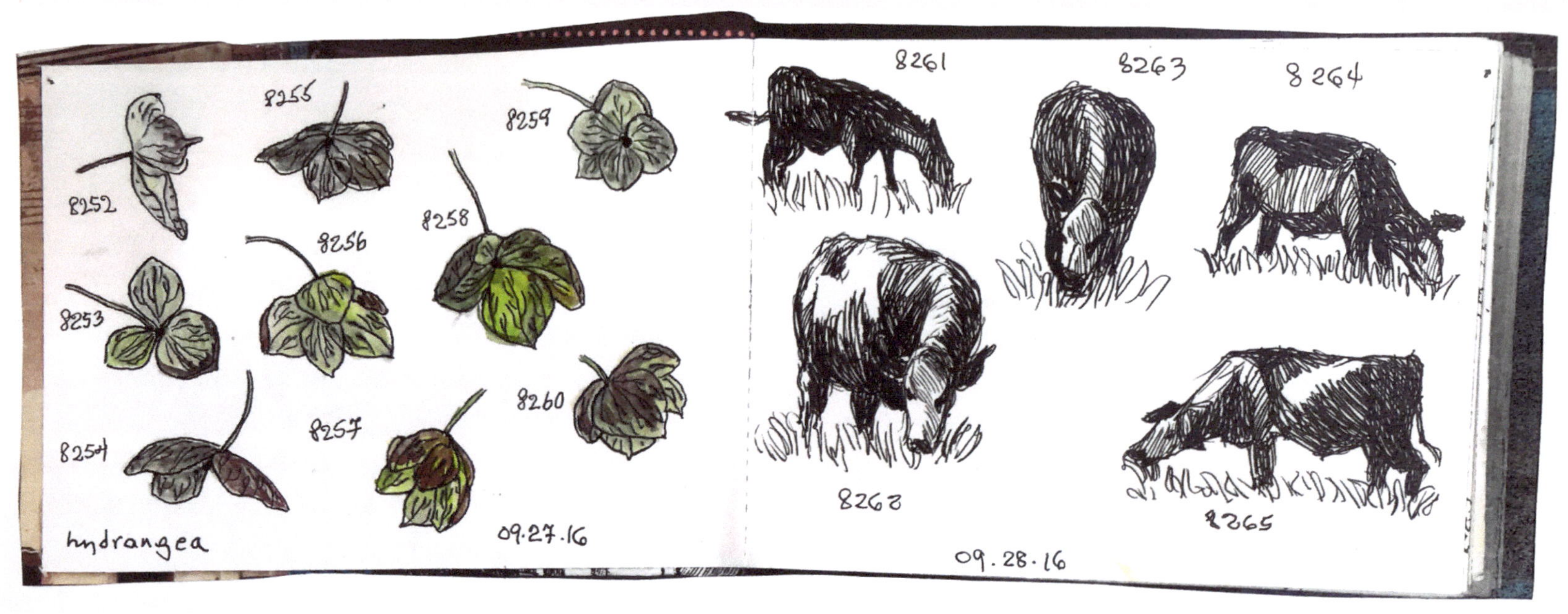

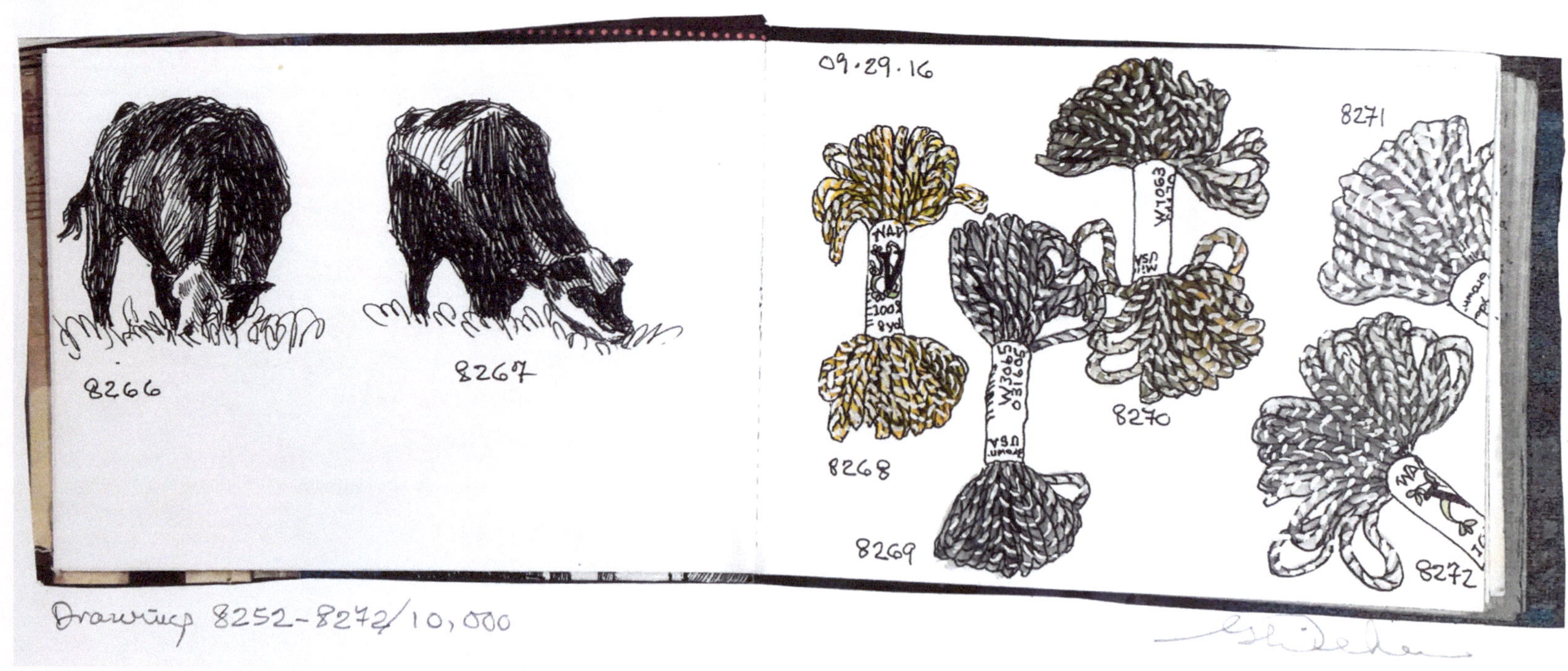

Drawings 8252-8272/10,000

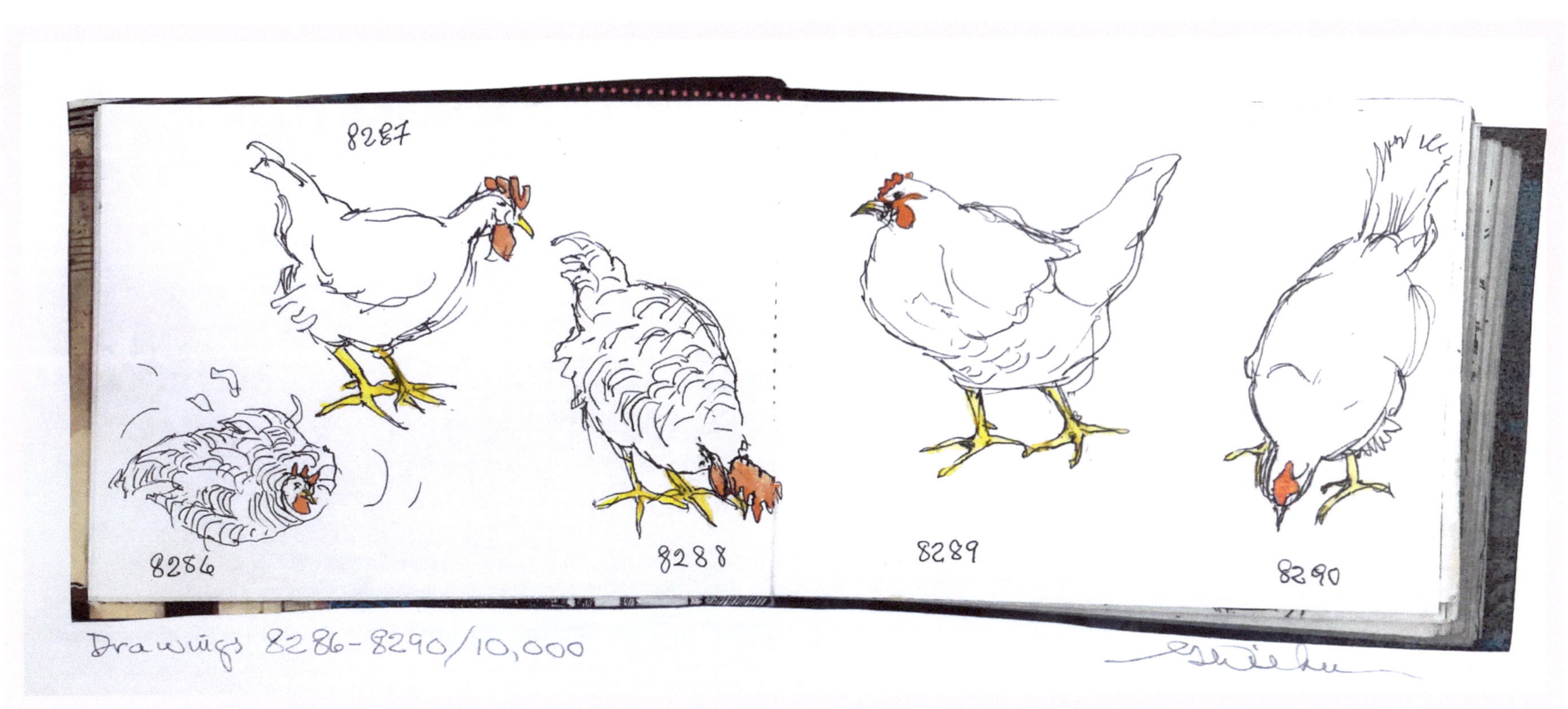

Drawings 8286-8290/10,000

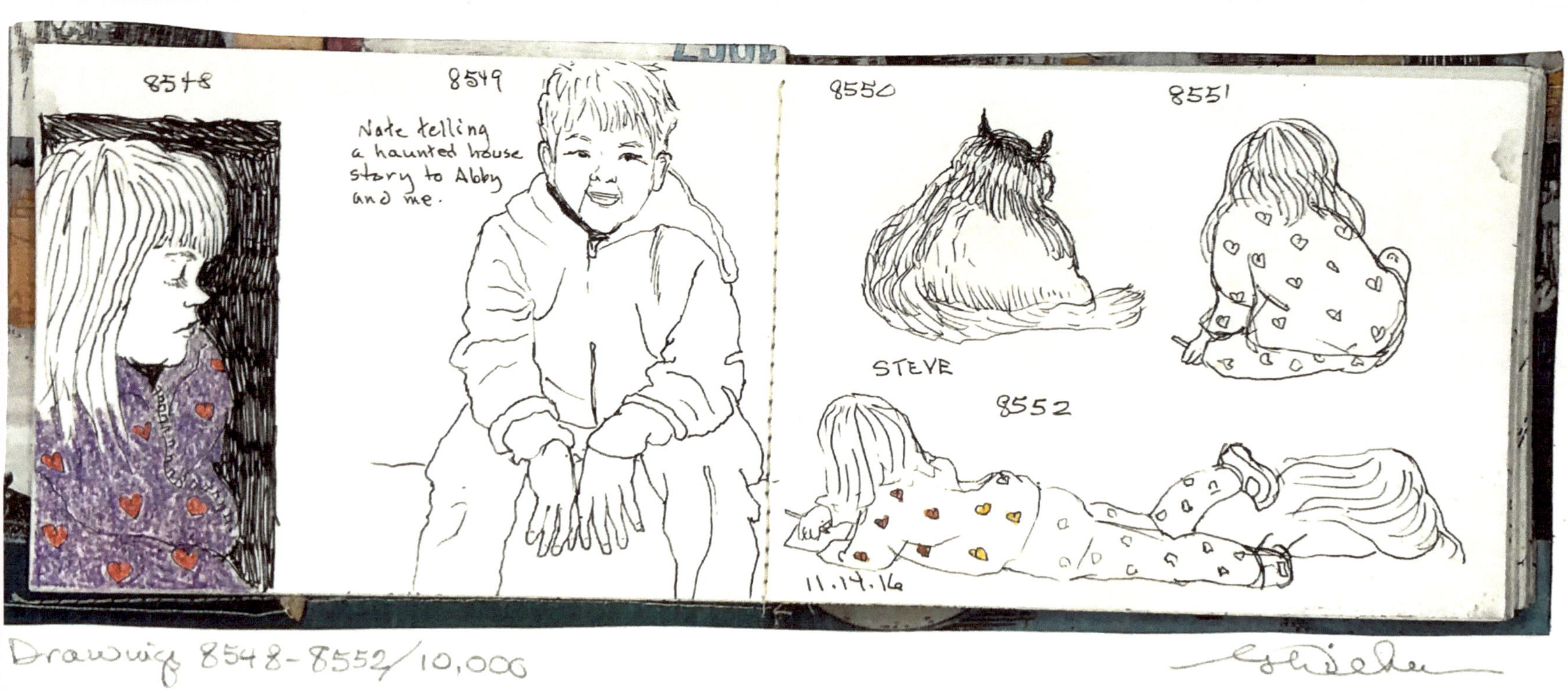

Drawing 8548–8552 / 10,000

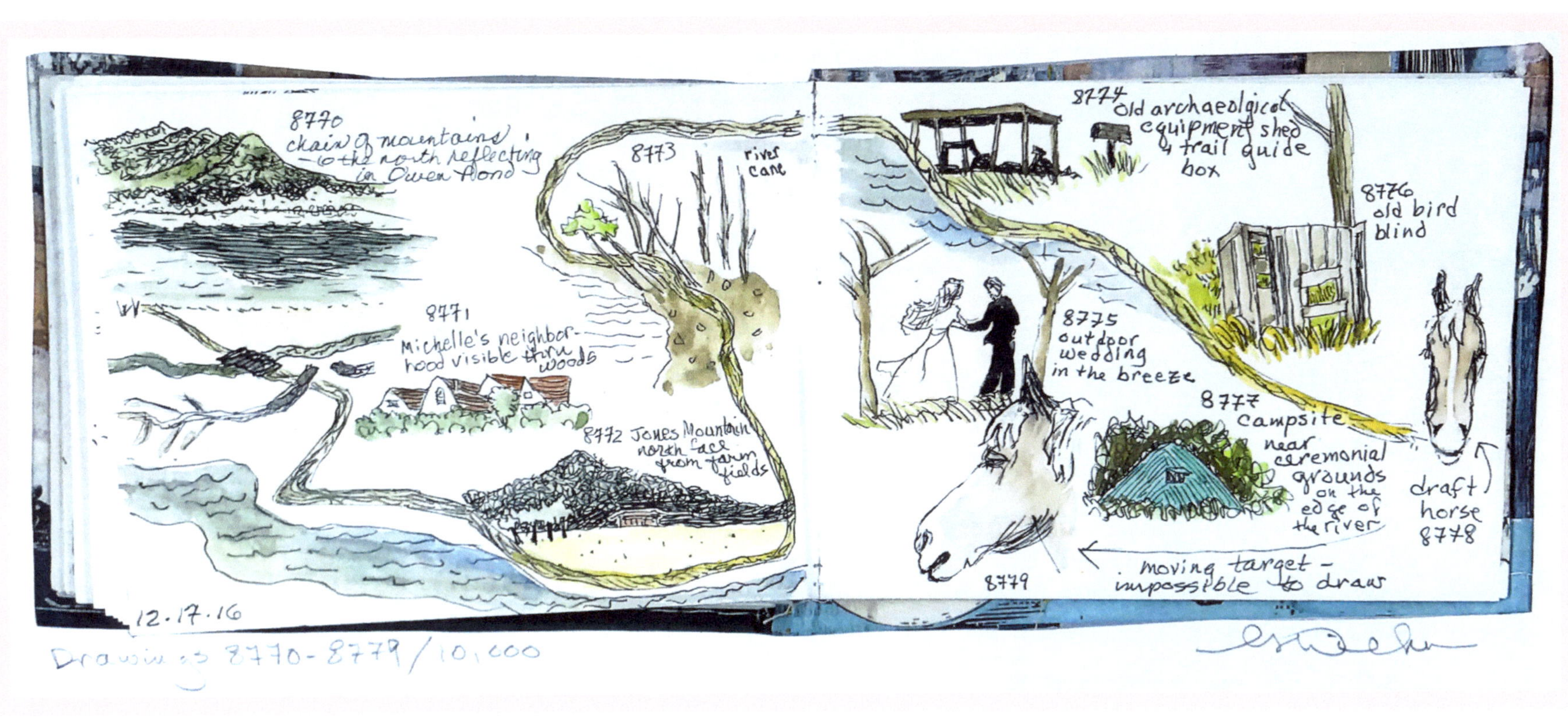

8770 chain of mountains to the north reflecting in Owen Pond
8773
river cane
8771 Michelle's neighborhood visible thru woods
8772 Jones Mountain north face from farm fields
8774 Old archaeolgical equipment shed & trail guide box
8776 old bird blind
8775 outdoor wedding in the breeze
8777 campsite near ceremonial grounds on the edge of the river
draft horse 8778
8779
moving target - impossible to draw
12.17.16
Drawings 8770-8779/10,000

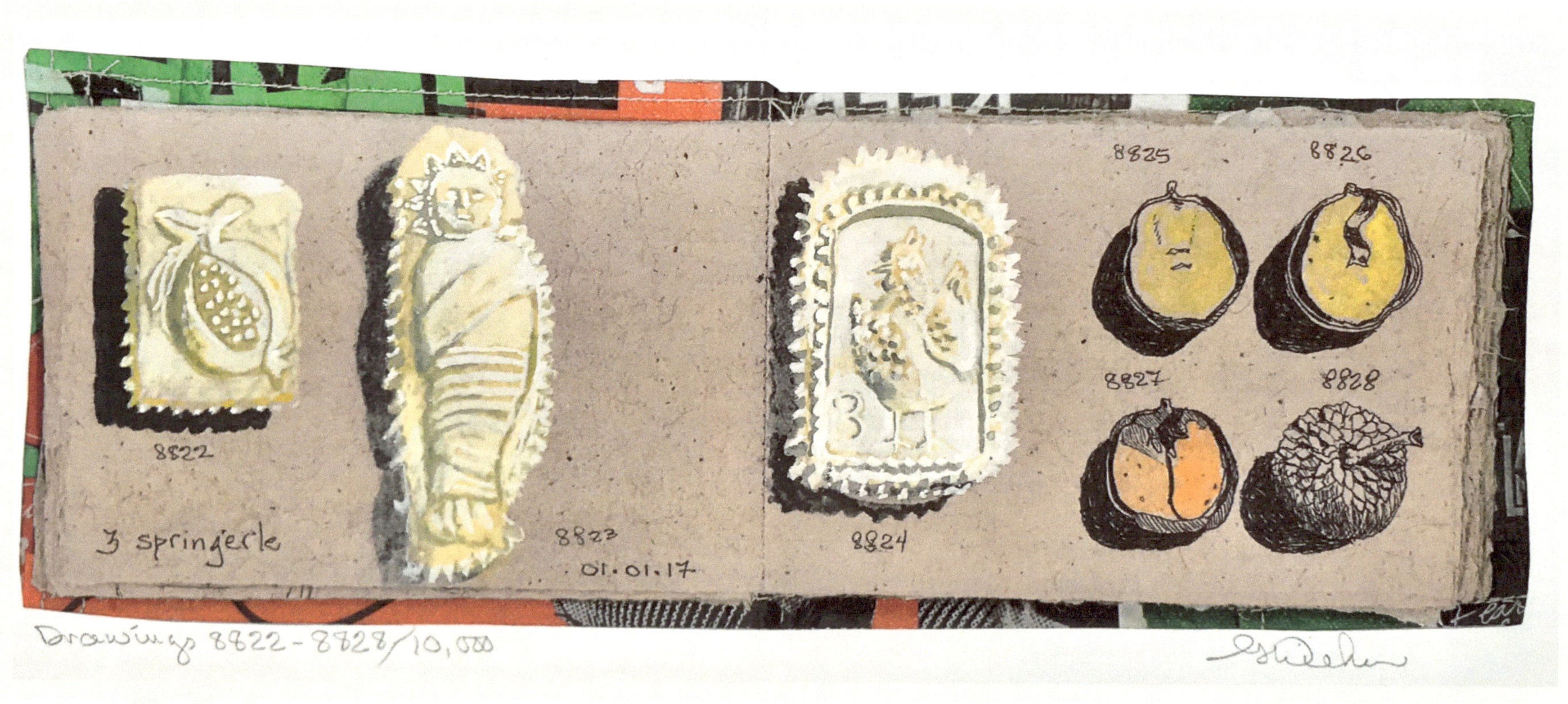

8822
3 springerle
8823
01.01.17
8824
8825
8826
8827
8828
Drawings 8822 - 8828/10,000

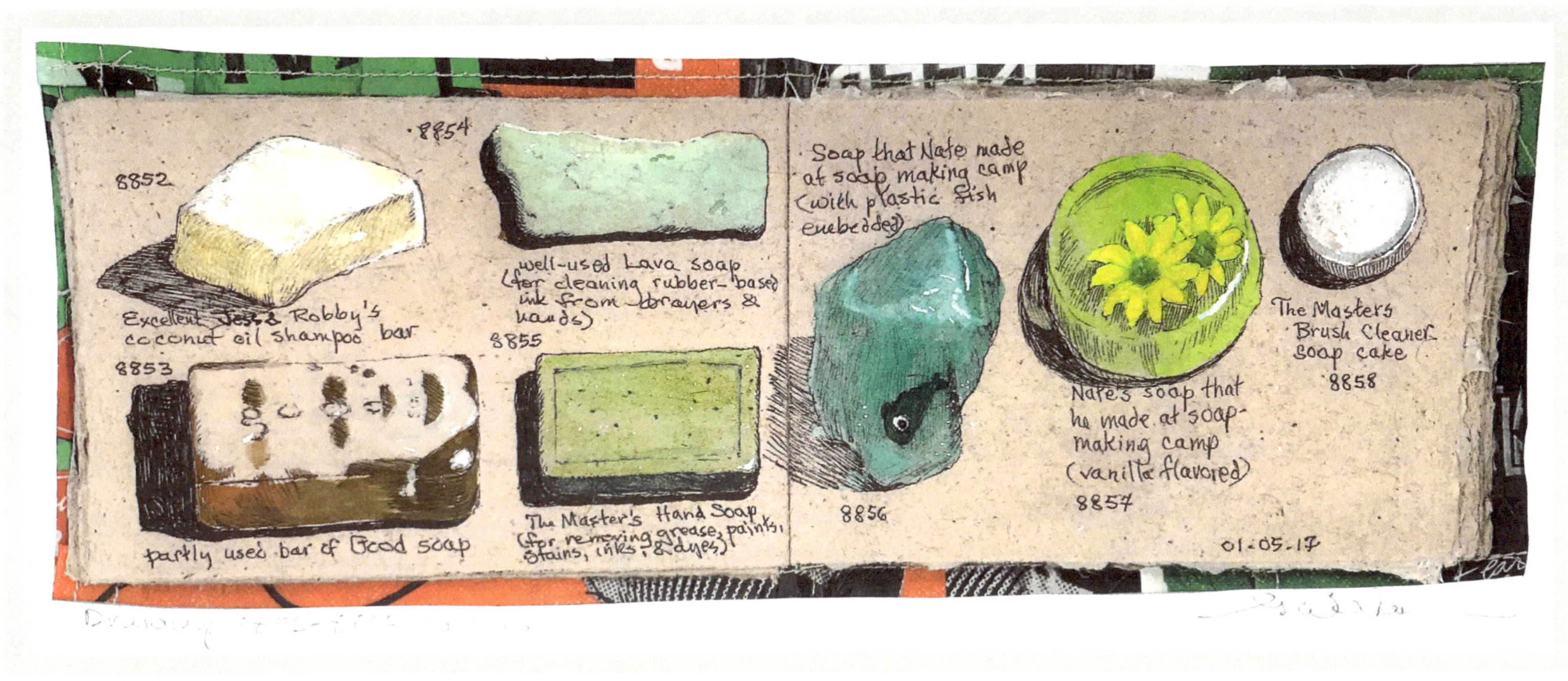

8852
8854
Excellent Jess & Robby's
coconut oil shampoo bar
8853
partly used bar of Good soap
well-used Lava soap
(for cleaning rubber-based
ink from brayers &
hands)
8855
The Master's Hand Soap
(for removing grease, paints,
stains, inks, & dyes)
Soap that Nate made
at soap making camp
(with plastic fish
embedded)
8856
Nate's soap that
he made at soap-
making camp
(vanilla flavored)
8857
The Masters
Brush Cleaner
soap cake
8858
01-05-17

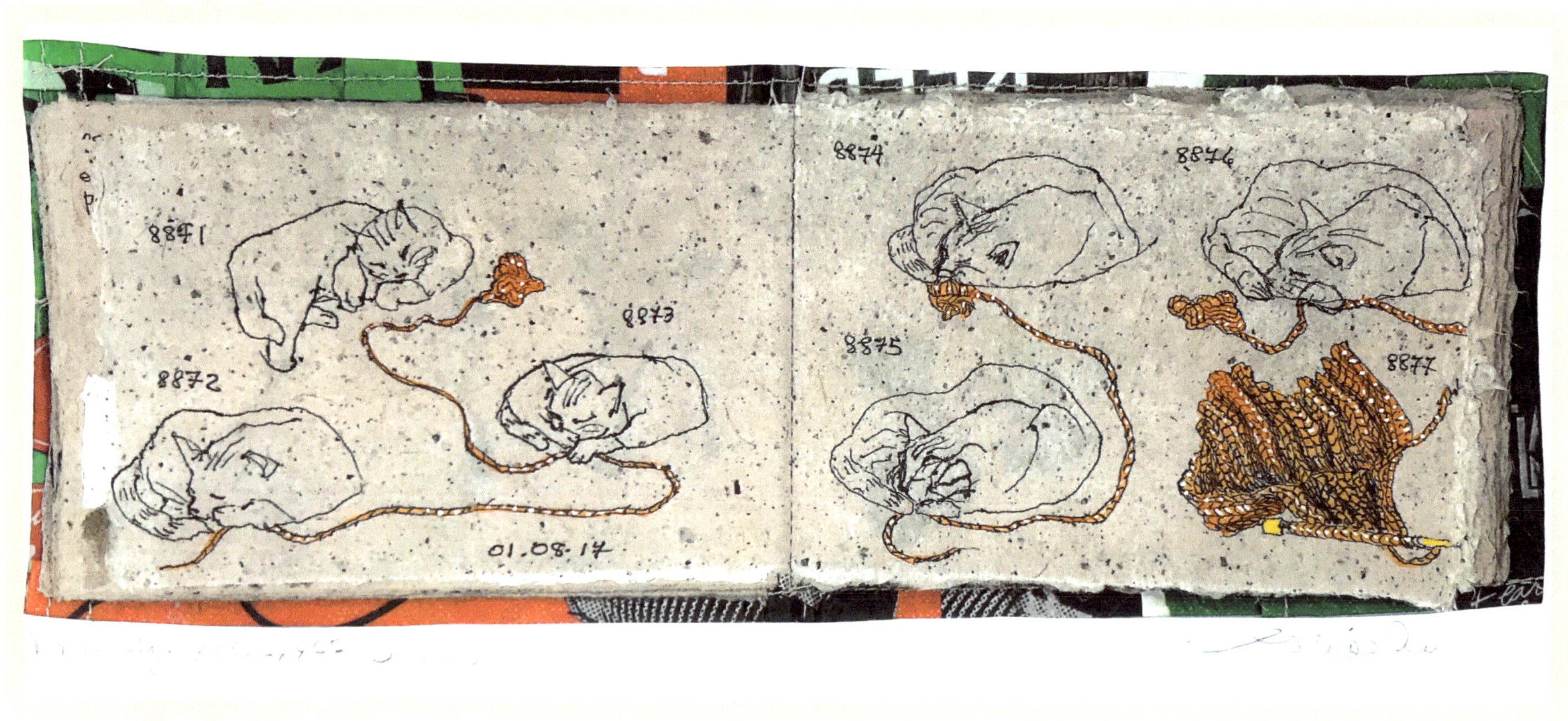

8871
8872
8873
8874
8875
8876
8877
01.08.17

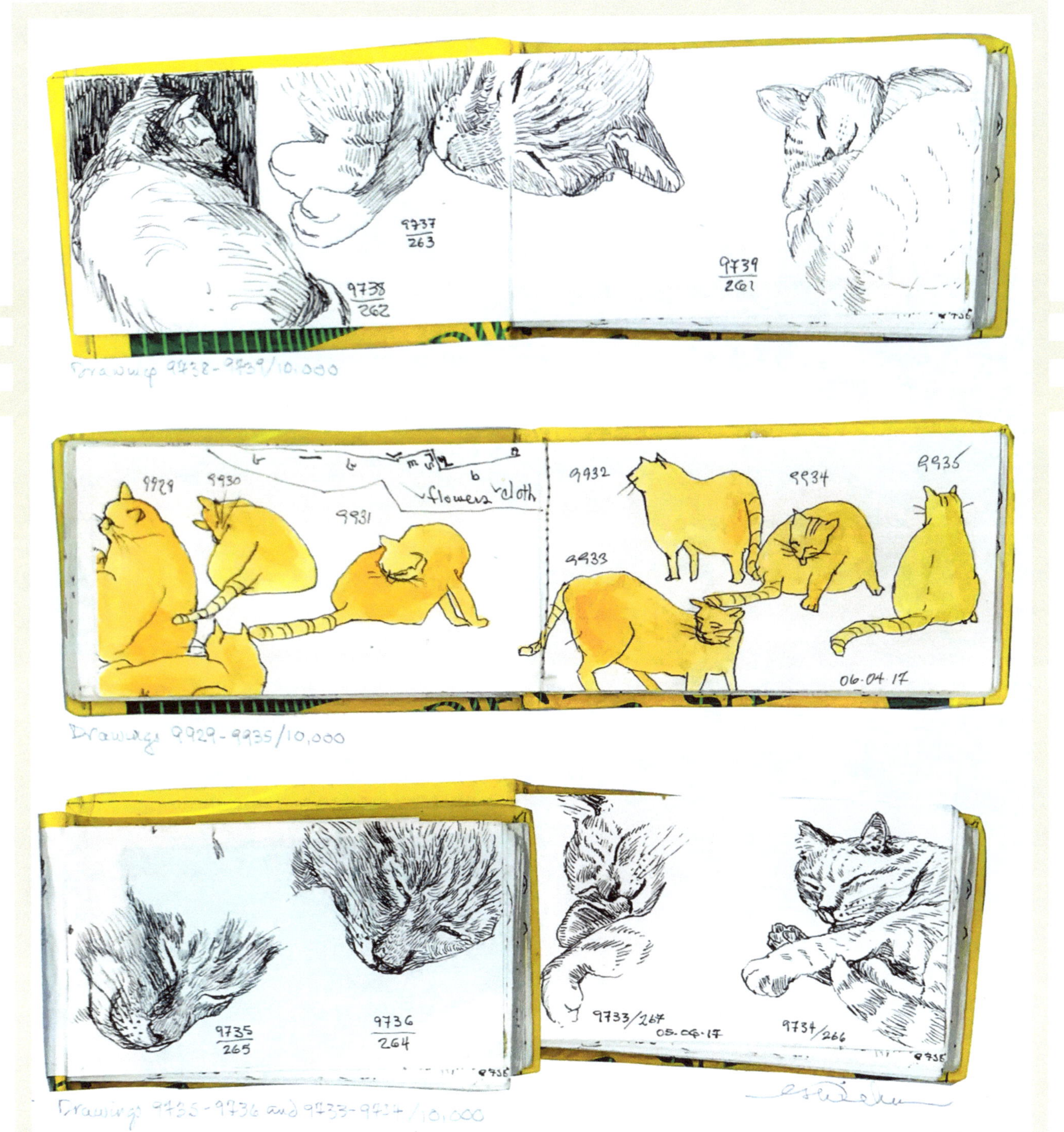

Drawings 9738-9739/10,000

Drawings 9929-9935/10,000

Drawings 9735-9736 and 9733-9734/10,000

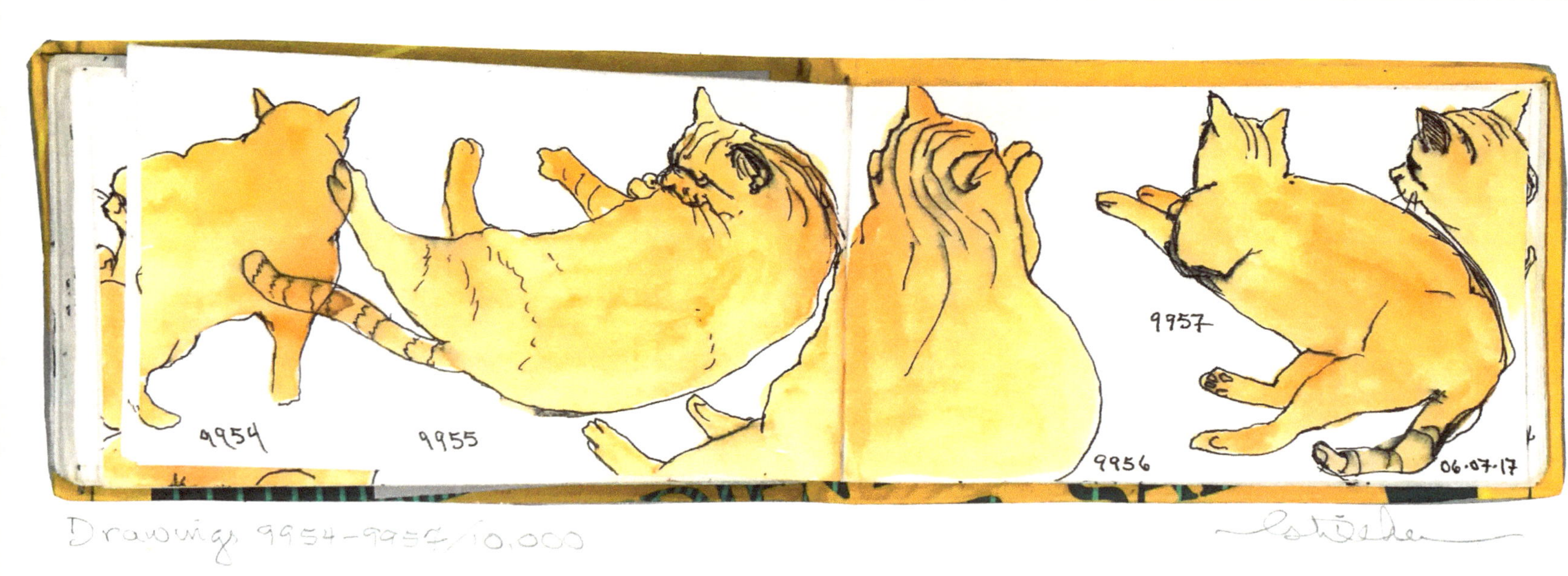
9954
9955
9956
9957
06-07-17
Drawing 9954-9957/10.000

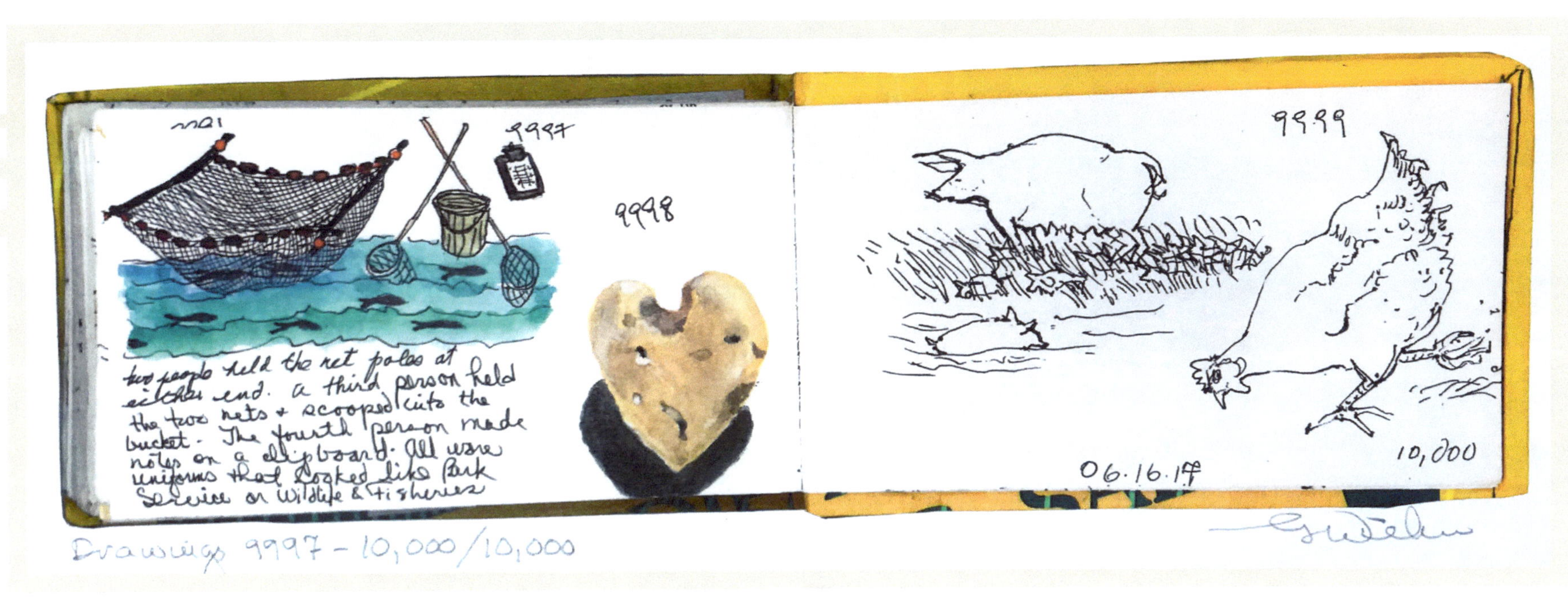

9997
9998
9999
two people held the net poles at
either end. a third person held
the two nets + scooped into the
bucket. The fourth person made
notes on a clipboard. All wore
uniforms that looked like Park
Service or Wildlife & fisheries
06.16.19
10,000
Drawings 9997 — 10,000/10,000

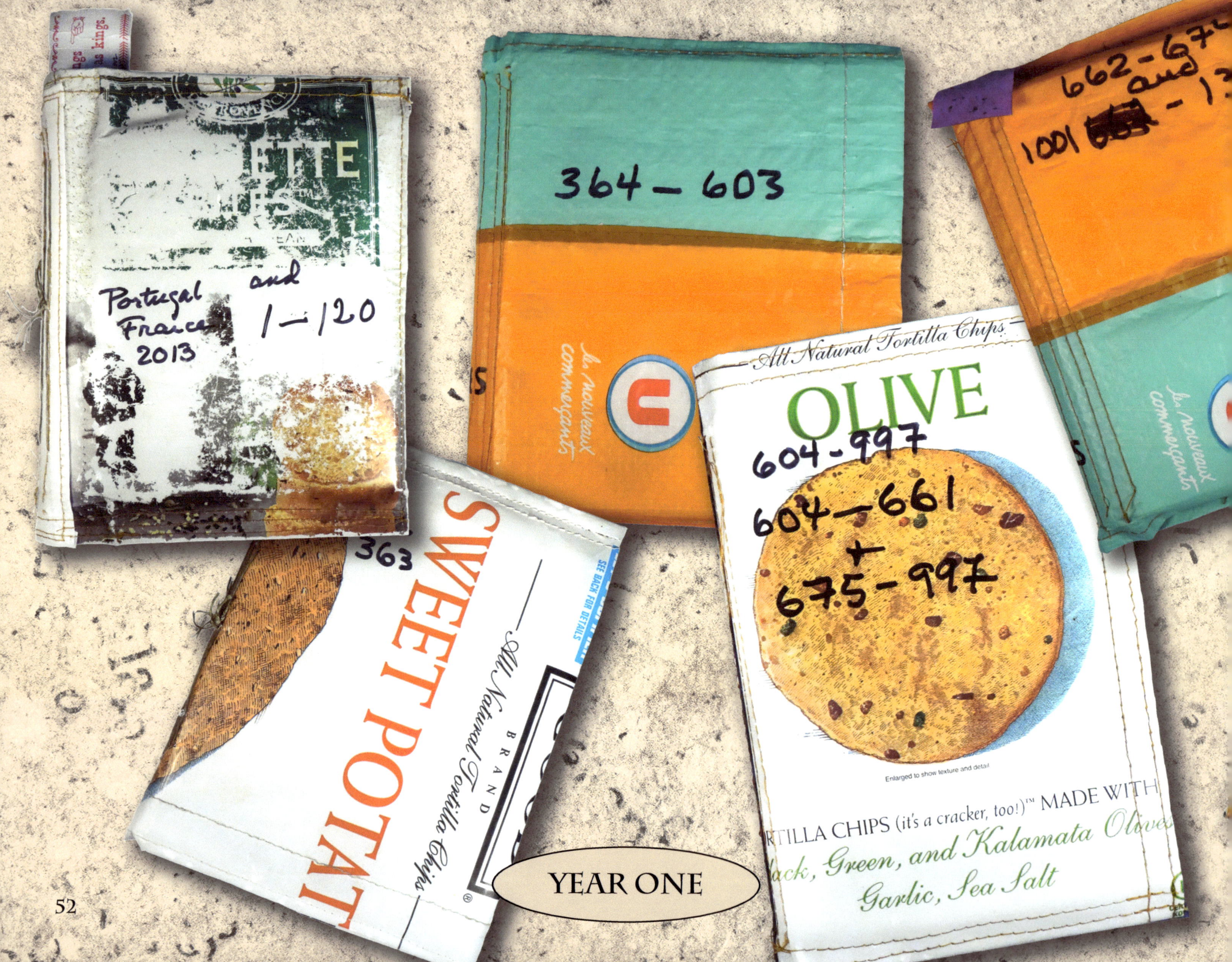
kings.
ETTE
Portugal and
France 1 - 120
2013
364 - 603
662 - 67
and
1001 - 13
La Nouveaux
Commerçants
All Natural Tortilla Chips
OLIVE
604-997
604 - 661
+
675 - 997
Enlarged to show texture and detail
363
SWEET POTAT
All Natural Tortilla Chips
BRAND
SEE BACK FOR DETAILS
La Nouveaux
Commerçants
TORTILLA CHIPS (it's a cracker, too!)™ MADE WITH
ack, Green, and Kalamata Olives
Garlic, Sea Salt
YEAR ONE

5TH SUN
SPECIALTIES
...VORS, NATURAL INGREDIENTS... REAL FOOD
MADE WITH ORGANIC BLUE CORN
cRc KOSHER 933
1355 - 1977
EP BLUE
WAY BETTE
SNACKS
SPROUT
25% LESS FAT THAN THE LEADING SWEET POTATO CHIP*
ORIGINAL
SWEET POTATO CHIPS
BRAND
FOOD SHOULD TASTE GOOD
See nutrition information for fat content
2018 - 2281
2013 - 14
HOMEMADE BUTTER
Batch...
"The Old Fashioned Way"
From Cows NOT Treated with Artificial Growth Hormone
KEEP REFRIGERATED
2 QUARTERS!
UNSALTED BUTTER
WORLD DAIRY EXPO FIRST PLACE
NET WT. 8 OZ 226g
FRESH FROM MAINE

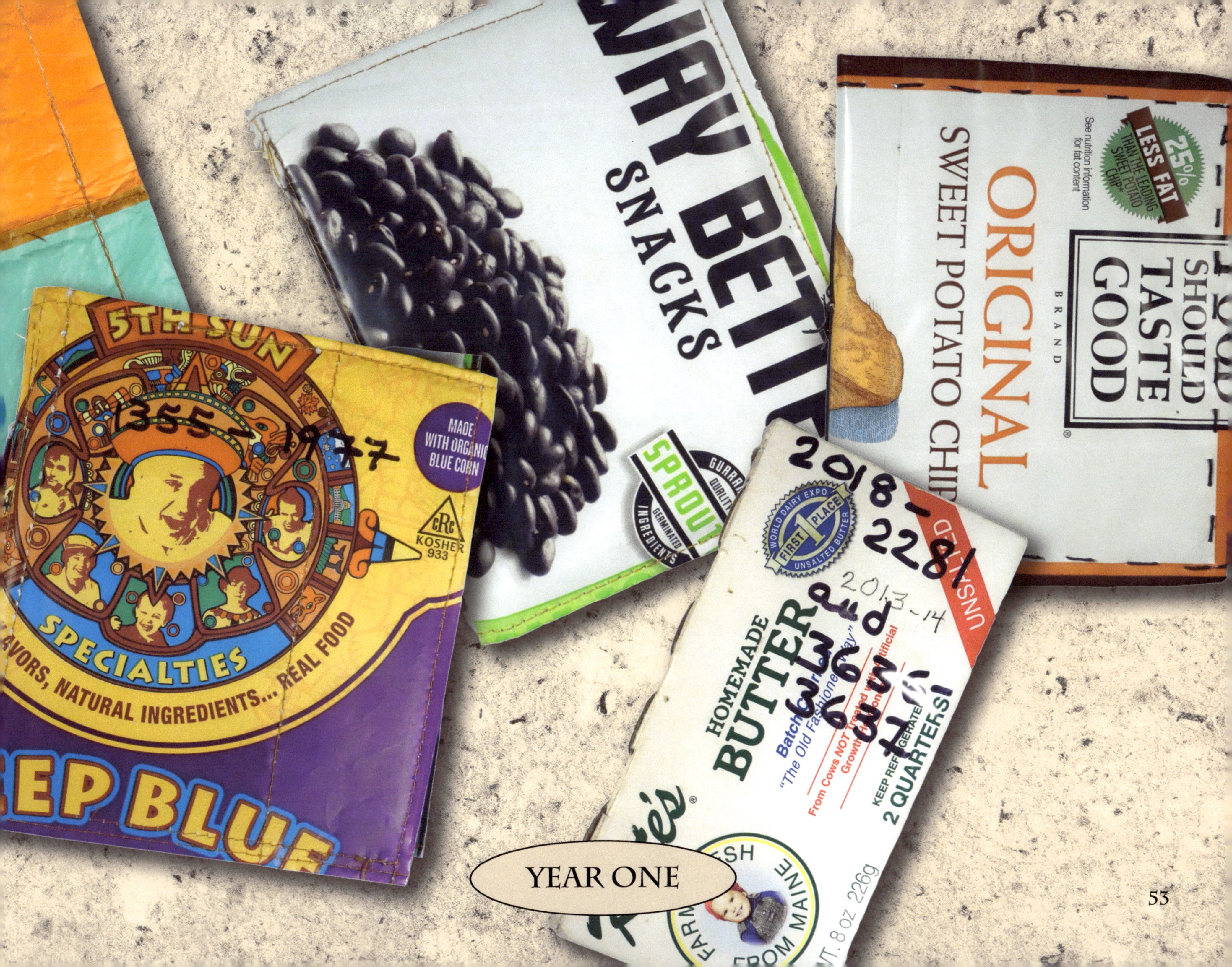

YEAR ONE

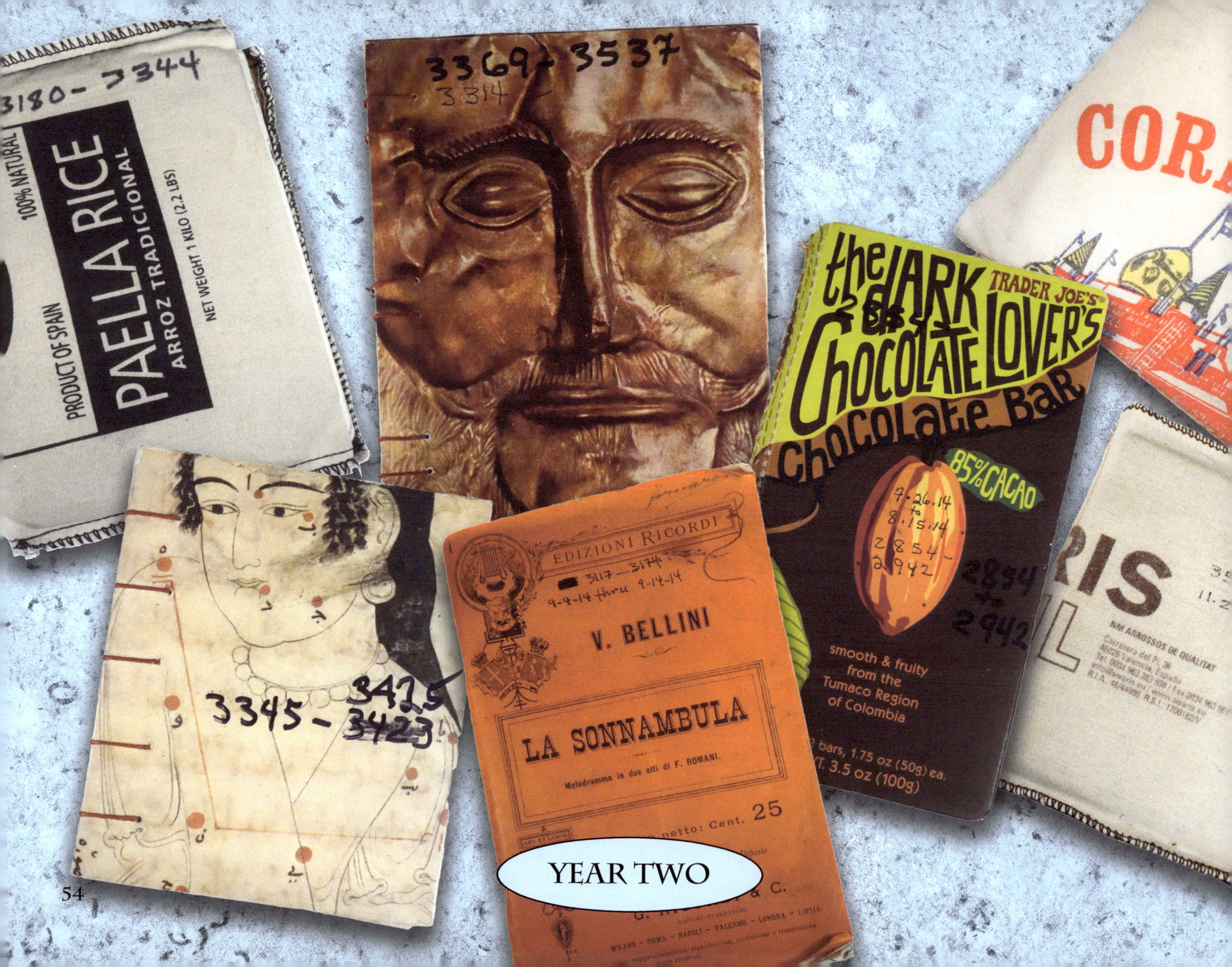
3180 - 7344
100% NATURAL
PRODUCT OF SPAIN
PAELLA RICE
ARROZ TRADICIONAL
NET WEIGHT 1 KILO (2.2 LBS)
3369 - 3537
3314
CORI
the DARK
TRADER JOE'S®
Chocolate LOVER'S
Chocolate BAR
85% CACAO
7-26.14
to
8.15.14
2854 -
2942
2854
to
2942
smooth & fruity
from the
Tumaco Region
of Colombia
2 bars, 1.75 oz (50g) ea.
NT. 3.5 oz (100g)
EDIZIONI RICORDI
3117 - 3174
9-4-14 thru 9-14-14
V. BELLINI
LA SONNAMBULA
Melodramma in due atti di F. ROMANI
netto: Cent. 25
ARS ET LABORE
YEAR TWO
G.
EDITORI-STAMPATORI
MILANO - ROMA - NAPOLI - PALERMO - LONDRA - LIPSIA
& C.
3345 - 3425
3345 - 3423
RIS
NM ARROSSOS DE QUALITAT
Carretera del Pi, 36
46026 Valencia, España
Tel. 0034 963 203 958 / Fax 0034 963 96
info@arrossos.eu / www.arsarros.eu
R.I.A. 55/44998 R.S.I. 1700182/V

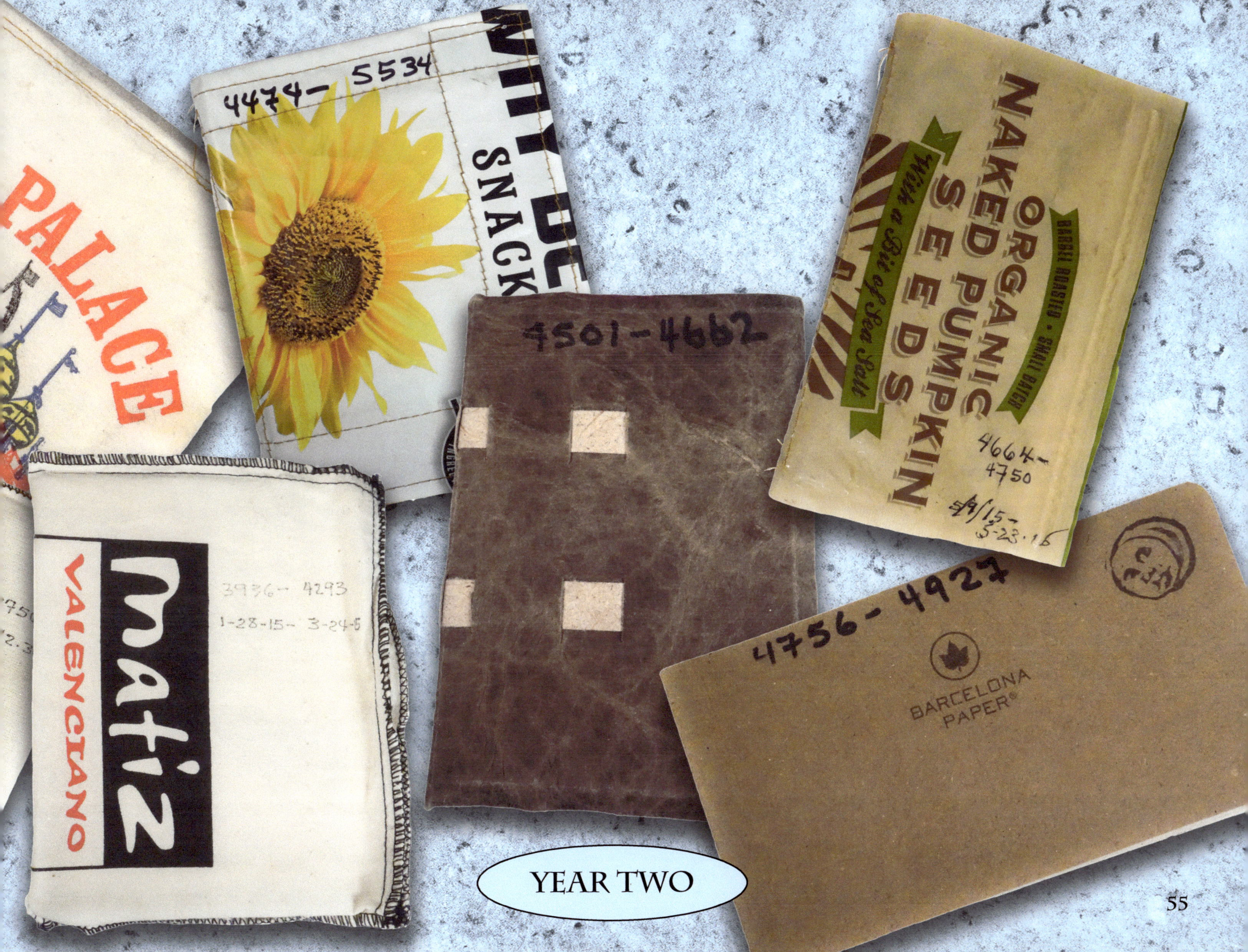
PALACE
VALENCIANO
matiz
4474 - 5534
SNACK
4501 - 4662
ORGANIC NAKED PUMPKIN SEEDS
BARREL ROASTED • SMALL BATCH
With a Bit of Sea Salt
4664 - 4750
5/9/15 - 5-23-16
3936 - 4293
1-28-15 - 3-24-5
4756 - 4927
BARCELONA PAPER
YEAR TWO

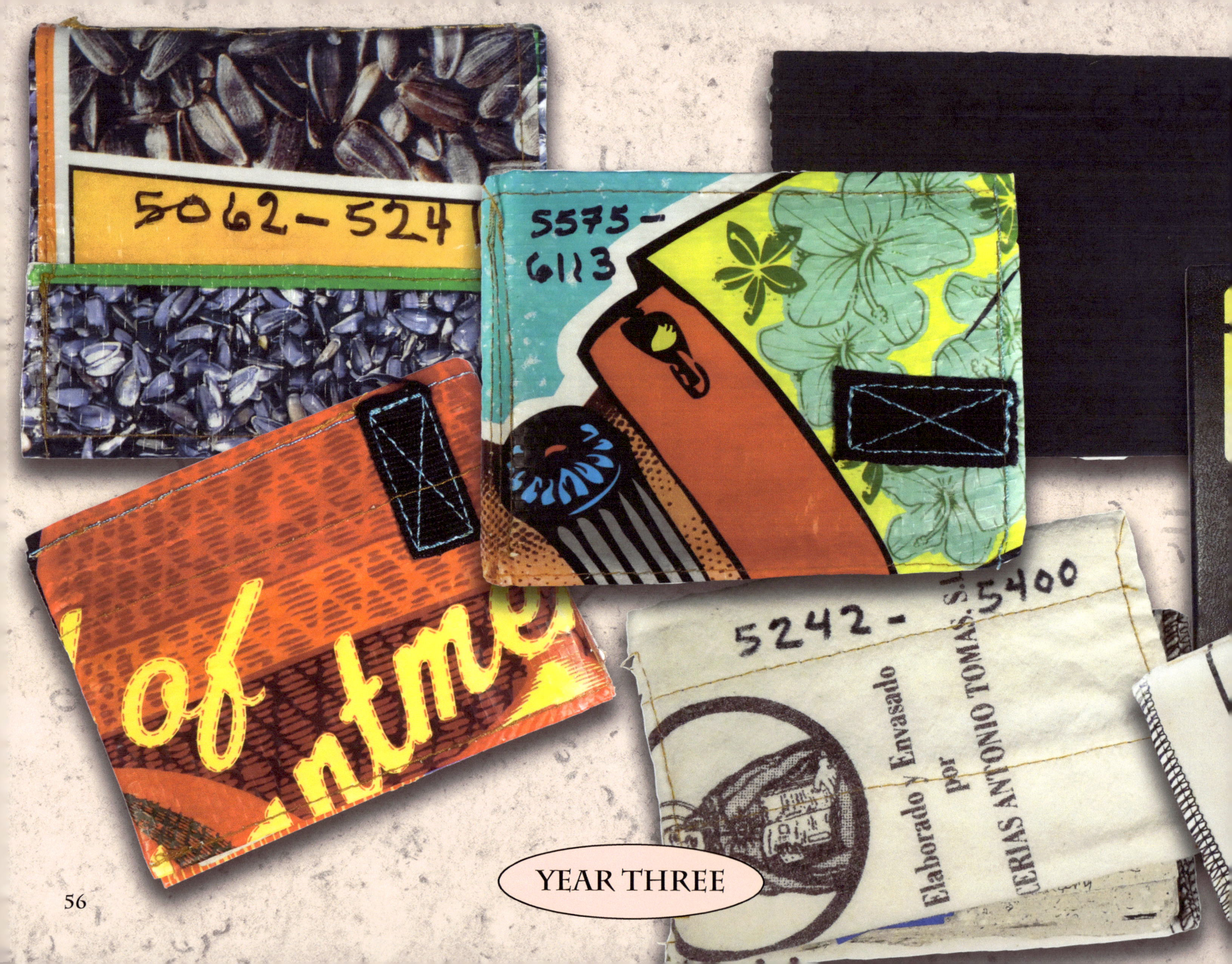

YEAR THREE

6686-
6765
Feb 2016 — March 2016
The Metropolitan Museum of Art New York
Quality Control H00308L
75-
653
7014-
7385
100% NATURAL
PRODUCT OF SPAIN
PAELLA RICE
ARROZ TRADICIONAL
NET WEIGHT 1 KILO (2.2 LBS)
6109-
6370
6765-
7013
T

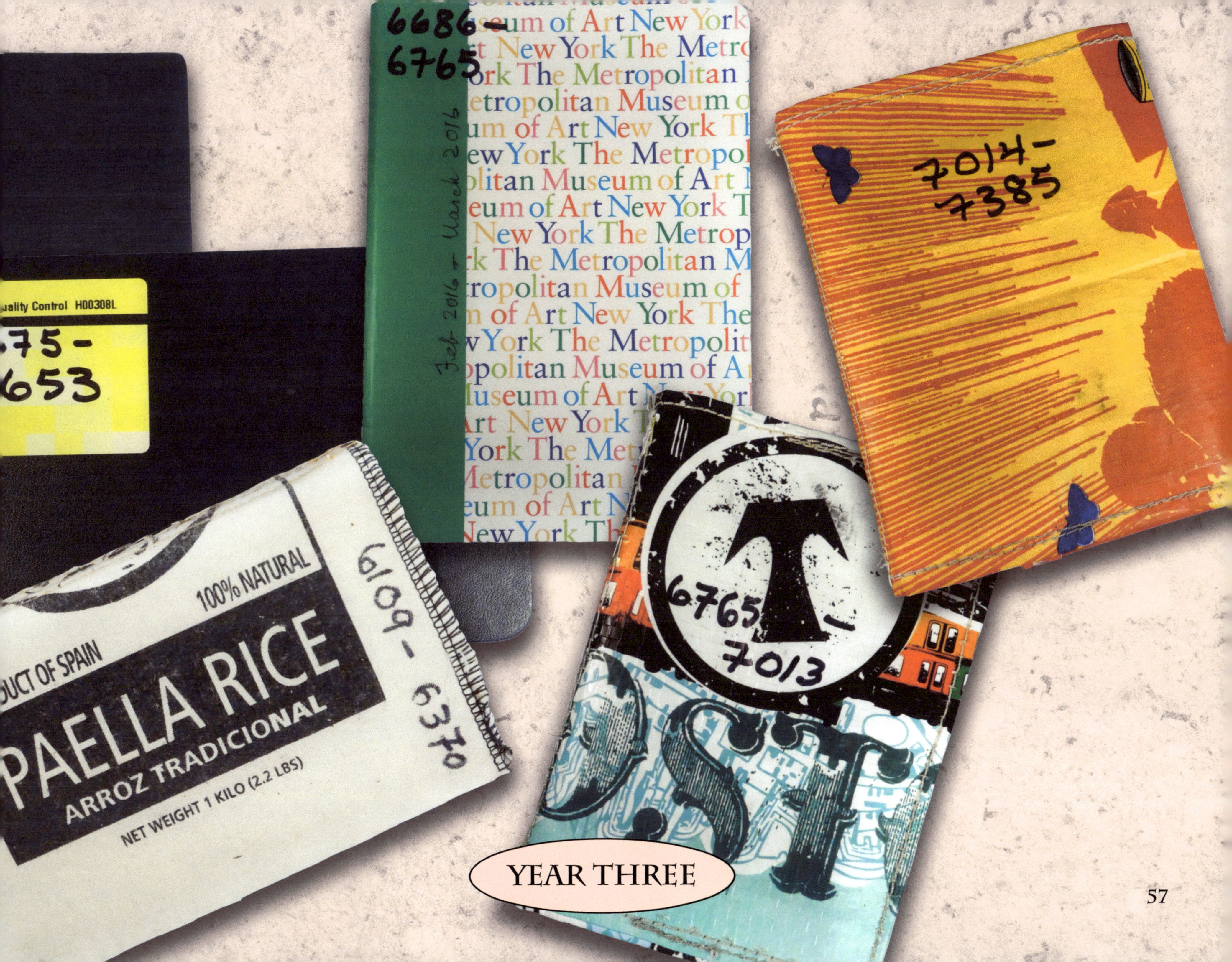

YEAR THREE

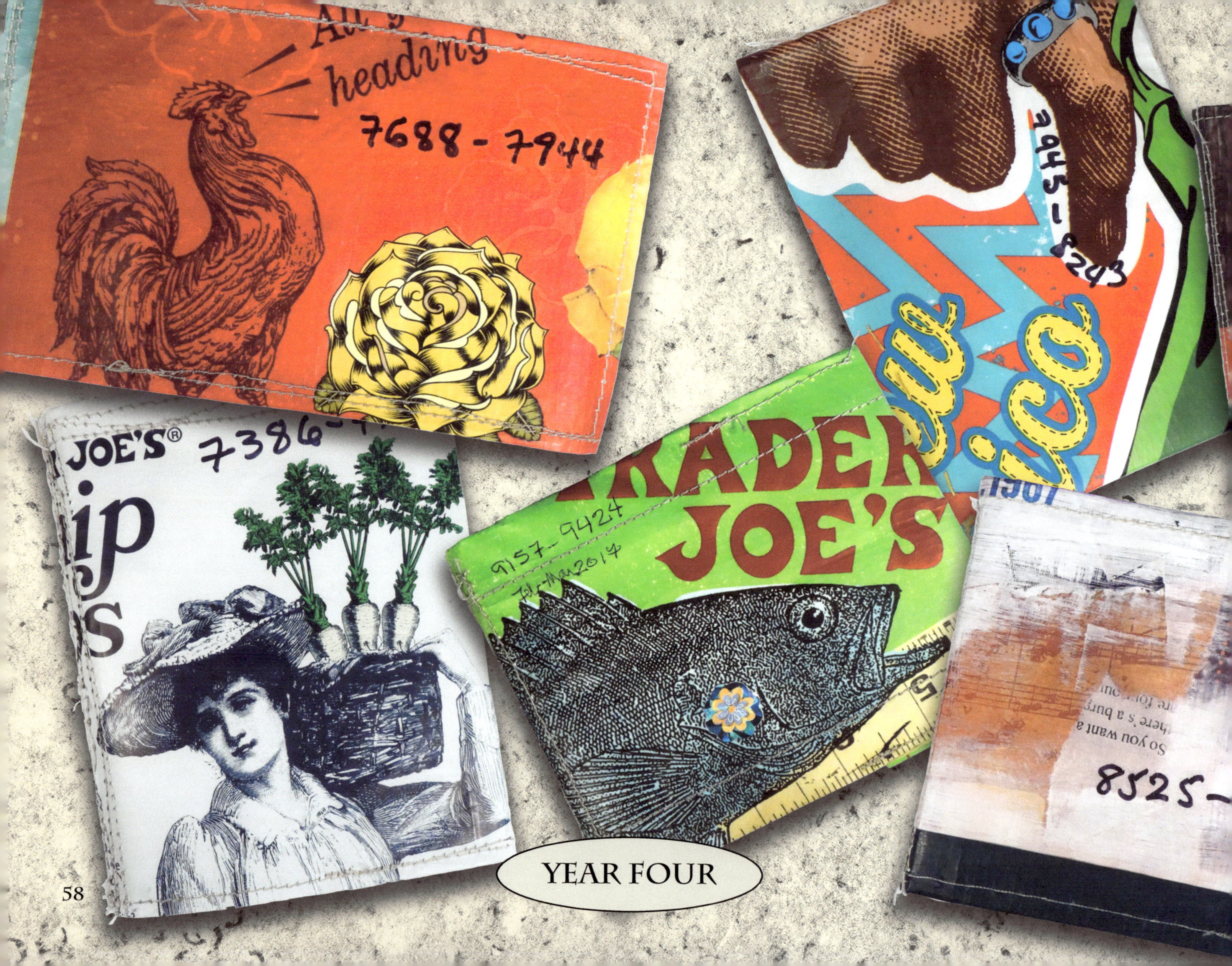

YEAR FOUR

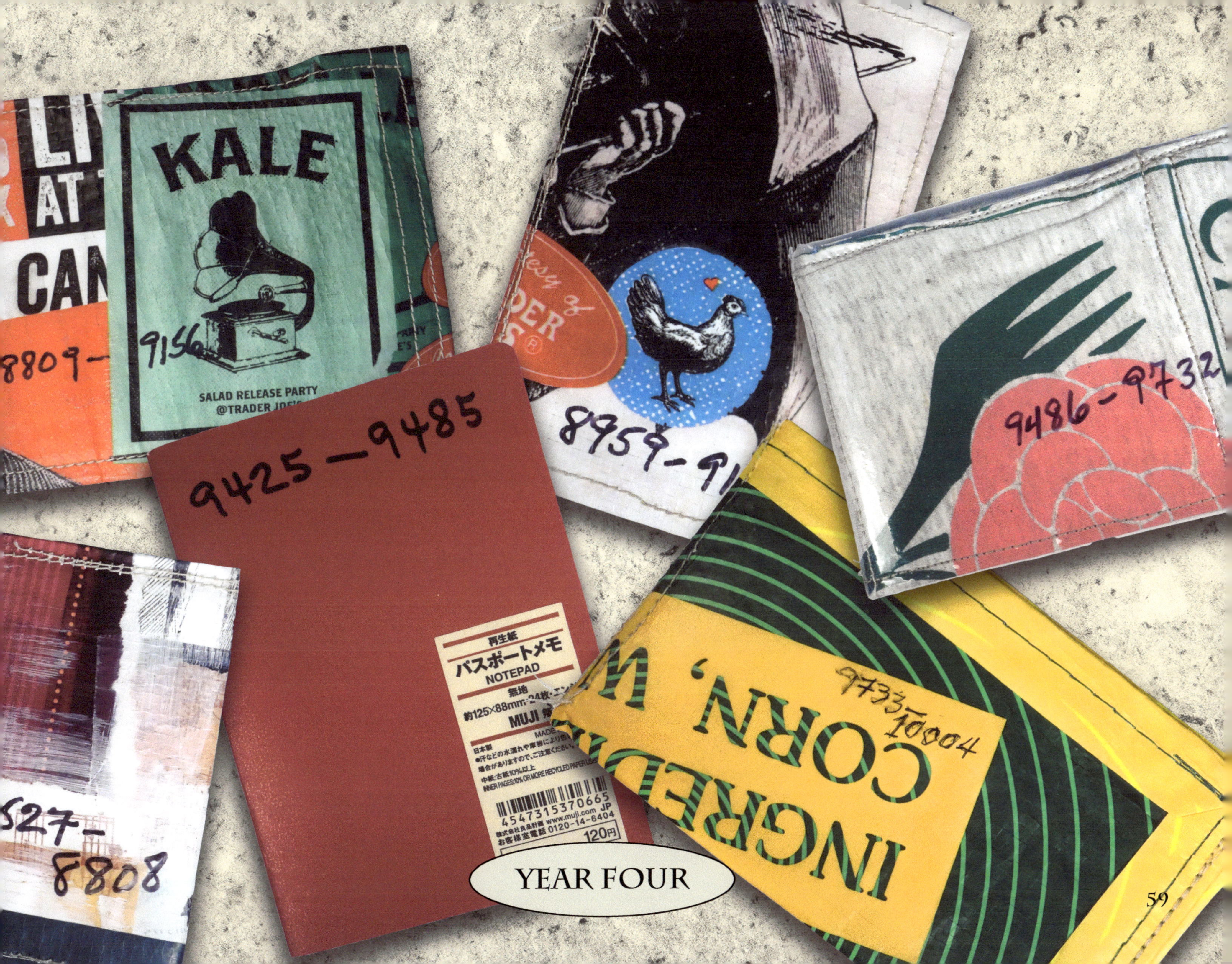
KALE
9156
SALAD RELEASE PARTY
@TRADER JOE'S
8809 -
9425 - 9485
8959 - 91
9486 - 9732
9733 - 10004
527 -
8808
再生紙
パスポートメモ
NOTEPAD
無地
約125×88mm 24枚
MUJI
日本製
4547315370665
www.muji.com JP
0120-14-6404
120円
CORN, W
INGRED
CORN'